HOW WE SEE OURSELVES

THE MODEL FOR LASTING RESULTS AND FULFILLMENT

BEN EDEN

Copyright © 2023 by Ben Eden

All rights reserved.

No portion of this book may be reproduced in any form without written permission from the publisher or author, except as permitted by U.S. copyright law.

Foreword

As a bestselling author and a speaker who has had the privilege of addressing audiences across the globe, I've encountered countless narratives about success, leadership, and personal transformation. However, it's rare to find a work that cuts to the very core of these topics with the clarity, insight, and actionable wisdom that Ben Eden's "How We See Ourselves" does. When Ben asked me to write the foreword for this masterpiece, I knew it was an opportunity to be part of something truly special.

In my travels—spanning over 300,000 miles a year—I've spoken to a myriad of individuals from diverse backgrounds, each on their unique journey towards self-improvement and leadership excellence. My book, "Doing What Must Be Done," has always been a beacon for those striving for greatness despite adversity. Ben Eden's "How We See Ourselves" is a luminous companion to this journey, shining a light on an aspect of success that many overlook: the power of self-perception.

The genius of Ben's work lies not just in its profound message but in the tangible tools it offers. Each chapter, a reflection of the table of contents I was fortunate to preview, serves as a stepping stone towards a transformative self-view. It's not merely about what we see in the mirror, but how that vision shapes our actions, decisions, and ultimately, our destiny.

Ben masterfully navigates through the intricate web of self-identity, belief systems, and the narratives we tell ourselves. He dissects the psychological barriers that hinder our progress and offers a blueprint for constructing a resilient, positive self-image. This book, in essence, is a mirror itself—one that reflects not who we are, but who we can become.

The power of "How We See Ourselves" is in its universal applicability. Regardless of where you are in your journey—be it a seasoned leader, a budding entrepreneur, or someone simply seeking personal growth—Ben's insights are invaluable. His writing resonates with a truth that is both timeless and timely: the foundation of all success is how we perceive ourselves.

In my years of speaking on leadership and self-improvement, I've emphasized the significance of mindset. Ben Eden's work not only echoes this sentiment but expands on it, offering a comprehensive guide to mastering the art of self-perception. This book doesn't just inspire change; it facilitates it.

As you turn the pages of "How We See Ourselves," you'll embark on a journey of introspection, discovery, and empowerment. Ben Eden has not only penned a book; he has crafted a mirror through which we can see our best selves. I am honored to introduce you to this transformative work, confident in its power to alter lives and reshape destinies.

Let this book be your guide as you navigate the complex, yet rewarding path of self-improvement. With Ben's wisdom as your compass, the journey towards a better, more successful you is not just possible—it's inevitable.

Chad Hymas

Best selling author and world renowned speaker

Contents

Chapter 1 - Less than 10%	4
Chapter 2 - Celebrating Wins	5
Chapter 3 - How We See Ourselves	7
Part 1 - The Eden Model	10
Chapter 4 - What is The Eden Model?	11
Part 2	37
Chapter 5 - Identity: How Do You See Yourself?	38
Chapter 6 - Belief: What Do You Believe About Yourself?	54
Chapter 7 - Thoughts: What Do You Think About Yourself?	74
Chapter 8 - Emotions: How Do You Feel About Yourself?	99
Chapter 9 - Behavior: How Do You Manage Your Behavior?	171
Chapter 10 - Results: What Results Do You Get?	192
Epilogue	194
Appendix	207
References	215

To those striving to be their best and to grow and contribute every day.

Thank you for reading this book. Thank you for allowing yourself to be inspired and take action based upon what you read and experience in this book. Thank you for sharing this book with others and causing it to impact thousands of people all over the world.

Thank you for being you.

As a result of reading this book, you will be able to master your thoughts of failure and shatter the chains of self-doubt. You will turn discouragement into passion that leads to growth. You will turn pain into power, fear into unstoppable confidence.

Believe in yourself, for within you lies an extraordinary force waiting to be unleashed. The time is now to Reach Your Ultimate Potential.

***

What you are about to read has the power to change you and the way you see your world. Are you ready?

CHAPTER 1 - LESS THAN 10%

Apparently, less than 10% of people read past the first chapter of a book.

CHAPTER 2 - CELEBRATING WINS

"Celebrate your wins. A win is a win. No matter how small."

Congratulations! You just read more of this book than 90% of people read in most books!

Throw your fist in the air and say, "Yeah!"

If you don't celebrate a win, the brain doesn't know it exists. In other words, you can continue reading and have nothing happen, or you can celebrate the fact that you just made it farther into a book than 90% of people and that is a big deal!

This book has the potential to make a powerful change in your life. But if you read it just to have something to read, you will miss out on its potential.

As Dale Carnegie once said in his book "How to Stop Worrying and Start Living",

> "Let me warn you: you won't find anything new here. But you will find much that is not generally applied." .... "Our trouble is not ignorance, but inaction."

So I invite you to read this book with a purpose. You will read a mix of stories and principles. All of it will be written for you, the reader.

At the end of each chapter, I will ask you some questions that will help you apply what you learn (not only from the words in this book, but from the thoughts you have as you read). I invite you to take time to answer these questions and take action on what you write down. As you do so, your confidence in how you see yourself and your future will grow.

Are you ready for that? If so, let's go!

Chapter 3 - How We See Ourselves

When an elephant is young, the trainer ties a metal chain around its ankle and attaches the other end to a metal pole in the ground. The little elephant looks at the restraint on its leg but doesn't think much of it and continues on as if nothing was there. It soon discovers the heavy chain is holding it back from moving away and spends an entire day trying in vain to pull itself free, only to be left with an injured and sore ankle.

The trainer comes back the next day, removes the metal chain, and replaces it with a rope. He then ties the rope to a wooden stake in the ground. The elephant looks down and thinks to himself, "Something is different!" It goes to move but finds that its ankle is still raw and it hurts too much to move. It looks down and thinks to itself, "There is something on my ankle. It hurts when I try to move; therefore I will not move."

The following day, the trainer returns and removes the wooden stake from the ground but leaves the rope around the elephant's ankle. The rope is still around the elephant's ankle, but it isn't tied to anything. The elephant looks down and thinks, "There is something on my ankle. It hurts when I try to move; therefore I will not move."

Fast forward 10 years to when the elephant is an adult. If the trainer places a rope around its ankle, the elephant will look down and think, "There is something on my ankle. *It hurt when I tried to move*; therefore I will not move."

As we look at this adult elephant we might think, "You are a massive beast with enormous strength and capability! That rope is tied to nothing! Why aren't you moving??" That is because, to the elephant, the rope represents years of unresolved emotional pain, unhelpful stories, and limiting beliefs. It now <u>sees itself as incapable</u> of moving because of the rope.

Are you someone who knows deep down that you have incredible potential like this elephant and yet you feel there something stopping you from being all you can be?

Have you ever seen yourself as less than you truly are? How has that affected your life? Your relationships? Your job? Your finances?

This book is for you if:

You are a driven high achiever... yet you are very self-critical and feel like things you do are never good enough. You don't like to fail. When you mess up you get really frustrated.

You want to make more of your life. You know you have more potential... yet you don't know where to start.

You have a history of success... yet you are worried about the future.

You have a talent for seeing what needs to be done and finding ways to fill that need... yet you are overwhelmed.

You are passionate about making a difference and creating something that helps others... yet you find yourself doing lots of things that are not your strengths nor your passion. You just want to do what you do best and be valued for it.

You are a leader... yet you feel overlooked. You know you are good at what you do. You have had great experiences and you are sure you could do extremely well when given other opportunities. And yet you see others who don't seem as qualified doing what you want to do.

You are trying your best... yet you feel undervalued. You aren't paid what you are worth, people aren't listening to your solutions, and it seems nobody cares about what you are doing. Your family doesn't understand, your friends don't relate, and you don't know what to do.

You are amazing... yet you are tired of feeling the way you do. You are lonely. You are frustrated that you aren't as happy as you'd like to be. You are frustrated that things aren't working like you want. You are afraid it will never get better and you don't even want to go there.

CHAPTER 3 - HOW WE SEE OURSELVES

Perhaps you have felt a lot of these and are so tired of being on the rollercoaster of emotions that you have become apathetic. You finally decided that you are tired of feeling the way that you do, so you decided it is easier not to care. You numbed your emotions. You numbed the pain.

You hate how you feel and you turn to your favorite coping mechanism to numb the pain and feel better. Sometimes you are desperate to end the emotional pain but you don't know how. Maybe you are ashamed of yourself because of the coping mechanisms you have turned to. You are tired of suffering in silence.

You think you are the only one that feels the way you do. Everyone else on social media seems to be growing and doing just fine! You do your best to make it look like you have everything put together - but you are suffering in silence.

You are ready to make a change!

You are ready to be honest with yourself and have a better life...

Is this you?

If so, I see you. I feel you. Everything is going to be ok.

We all go through something like this elephant did - but at varying depths throughout our lives.

Think of it, have you ever felt like you were stuck in a situation that you couldn't control? That no matter what you did, you couldn't break free from the chains that held you down?

Have you ever struggled with self-doubt and inadequacy? If so, you're not alone.

Unlike the elephant, you can come to realize that you are not chained to anything. You can learn to see yourself for who you truly are. You can discover your true potential and learn to live up to it.

PART 1 - THE EDEN MODEL

Chapter 4 - What is The Eden Model?

The Eden model came to me after hundreds of hours of coaching my clients.

Everyone who has achieved lasting results and fulfillment has followed the Eden Model. Failure to follow the Eden Model the right way leads to doubt, frustration, and lack of fulfillment.

I will first illustrate how most people (including the elephant) go through this model backwards and therefore doubt themselves because of a lack of results.

After we finish in this direction, I will show you how using the model the right way is a more powerful and sustainable way of getting the results you want.

The Model Backwards

Here is the model as most people see it.

Starting from the top, the world teaches us to prioritize results. Whenever you start something, you start with a desired result.

What do you want?

Maybe you want to lose weight, earn money, grow your business, grow your family, etc.

For this example, let's talk about making money as a result.

So you want to make more money. Great!

Now that you know what you want, you begin to take the necessary steps towards achieving it. We all know that behaviors lead to results.

What must you do to get that result?

You decide to try a few things to make more money.

Let's say whatever you try doesn't work.

So you try a few more things and still don't get the result you want.

Now you start to experience a bunch of emotions.

How do you feel?

You are confused and frustrated because it isn't working.

You start to worry it won't work.

CHAPTER 4 - WHAT IS THE EDEN MODEL?

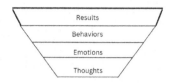

What do you think about it?

You start to think this is too hard and you wonder if you should just give up. You begin to believe you will never make more money.

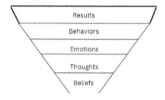

What do you believe about it?

You believe you don't deserve more money anyway. Making money is too hard.

And finally, you think you just weren't cut out for this anyway.

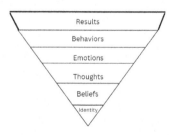

How do you see yourself?

Now you say you aren't a money maker. You aren't like those other people that have money.

Do you see how this works and how quickly it can happen? You have this idea or this desire and you decide to go for it. After a while, you not only give up on the idea but you begin to give up on yourself.

This is exactly what happened to the elephant. He wanted to move around but he tried and tried and it didn't work. He got discouraged. He thought it hurt too much. He stopped believing it was possible and he doubted himself so much that he stopped trying.

Let's observe this backwards (or upside-down) model a little more and realize what is happening.

We'll continue to use the example of making more money. This time we will be a little more specific.

So you want to make more money?

You might begin by thinking, "I'm going to look on Facebook and see what the strategy of the day is. I'm going to see what somebody else has done and then try that...."

Or you look for the quick fix, the miracle pill, the perfect strategy, the silver bullet, or whatever behavior is most likely to get you more money as quickly as possible (because why wait when you want it now, right?).

If you are lucky enough to find (and have the money to pay for it) the perfect solution, you will get the result you want and you will be happy! You are happy, proud, and ready to keep doing whatever you are doing to get more money. You chalk this behavior up to be a success and something you can use and rely on for the future.

But what if that behavior doesn't get you the result you want? What if it fails?

You might think, "If at first you don't succeed, try, try again!" But you can't try the same thing because "Doing the same thing over and over in hopes to get a different result is the definition of insanity." So you feel you have to try something else in hopes that it works. You know how it is. You work harder, longer, faster, invest more, etc. And you stay in this cycle until you finally find something that works or until you lose patience, get frustrated, discouraged, anxious, etc., and end up giving up on whatever it is you were trying to do.

CHAPTER 4 - WHAT IS THE EDEN MODEL?

Now we go deeper, to the level of emotions.

This is the part we don't always talk about, but we are emotional beings and every behavior is based on an emotional need.

We do things because we "feel like it." Or we do things until we don't "feel like it" anymore. Can you relate?

If you like how you feel, you do more of the same behavior to keep feeling that way, ie, you get complimented after providing service to someone so you keep providing service.

If you don't like how you feel, you find something else to do so you no longer feel that way, ie, you were embarrassed the last time you went to a networking meeting, so you don't go to them anymore.

Up to this point, your brain is saying, "I want to make more money, so I am going to put myself out there and ask for it."

But here is a question you ask yourself whether verbally or not:

"Do I feel like it? Do I feel like putting in this effort?"

You want to make more money, right? You have to make sales. You have to talk to people. You have to provide value.

If you say to yourself, "I just don't feel like it today. I'm just not feeling motivated." Are you going to do the work? Nope.

Then you wonder why you didn't meet your goals.

Why don't we realize what is going on here? Because we're just not used to talking about it. We're used to ignoring emotions or turning to our coping mechanisms because we just don't want to address those emotions.

The next step in this backwards model is the idea of our thoughts.

We all have thoughts, but unless you learn to be mindful and observe your thoughts, you don't realize what's going on. You just think, "That's life and I have no control over it."

You are continuously having a conversation in your mind about where you are in relation to your desired result.

If you are getting the results you want, you get excited and start to have all these exciting and positive thoughts about how well this is working, how good you feel, and how you are going to keep doing this and can't wait to do the next thing.

If you aren't getting the result you want, you have a conversation in your head about how frustrated you are and you wonder if it will ever work.

This is where a spiral happens. Most people live in their thoughts or live inside their heads and get stuck there because they are not connecting with the right emotions to get the results they want. Often it is a circular process that keeps you spinning in place.

You want to make more money. So you put yourself out there. Occasionally you feel motivated enough to put in the effort.

All this is based on thoughts. These thoughts become stories that you tell yourself - conversations that you have in your head. *"I think I can make this work. It makes sense and would be worth the effort. Someone else said that it could work, so I'm going to give it a shot."*

This is often as deep as most people consciously go.

But there are two more steps and they are very closely related.

Let's go to the next level down, to another level that most people don't think about because this is in the subconscious.

What is your belief about the situation?

What's your belief about money in general? Are you worthy of money? Can you get the money? Is this too hard? Will this ever work?

These are the thoughts you have that reveal your beliefs about the situation.

A belief is a feeling of certainty. It comes from repeated conversations you have had with yourself. Things you continuously say to yourself. Do you believe it is possible?

All the levels of the model so far are based on the results that you get or that you see.

I put in the effort (behavior). Did I get the results? Did I make money?

Yes or no?

How do I feel (emotions) about my results?

If I got the money, "Hey! I feel good!"

CHAPTER 4 - WHAT IS THE EDEN MODEL?

If I didn't get the results? "Man! This sucks!"

Then I experience a bunch of thoughts.

If I got the money: "Yay! This is incredible! I'm so happy it worked out. I can keep doing this for a long time!"

If I did not get the money: "Shoot. Is this for me? Is this going to work? I don't know how much longer I can keep doing this. I am going to have to find another solution."

This is all creating and based on the beliefs that we have.

The thoughts and feelings we experience repeatedly can gradually become our beliefs. "I'm not up to it. It's a failure. I'm sure it won't work out." Then when it doesn't work out, our brain says, "See? I told you so!" and it reinforces the belief.

What this all comes down to is your identity - or how you see yourself. The model followed in this direction makes your identity contingent upon your results.

If you don't get the results you want, you are frustrated and doubt every part of the process.

The biggest doubt and frustration falls on how you feel about yourself. You, subconsciously at first, wonder if there is something wrong with you and if you are good enough to ever get the result you want.

You start to see yourself differently.

Here is what happens inside your brain in this case:

At first, you thought, "Yeah, I can make money! I think I am capable."

Then you think, "I didn't get the outcome I was hoping for. Trying this approach didn't have the effect I wanted. This is feeling kind of pointless. I'm not sure this will be successful. I don't think I'm good at making money. I just don't think I am cut out to be a money maker."

Have you ever had one of these thoughts?

Have you ever secretly wondered, "Why can't I get this to work?" Or "Am I cut out for this?"

When your sense of identity wavers, you begin to question your abilities.

***

Here is the model in its simplest form:

EITHER:

> <u>It works</u>
> Repeat the behavior
> Feel excited it is working
> Can't wait to tell everyone about it
> Become confident in your ability to get results
> Begin to see yourself as successful

OR

> <u>It doesn't work</u>
> Try to force the behavior or give up
> Feel depressed, frustrated, and ashamed it isn't working.
> Don't want to talk to anyone about it
> Wonder if this will ever work
> Begin to doubt your ability to get results

Every layer is completely dependent upon the results. If they are satisfactory, everything else will look great. If not, everything else is a bust and so are you. You feel like a failure and believe the world judges you the same way. You think your outcomes determine your worth in the world. Your sense of identity is contingent upon your results. Therefore, the model in this direction works for you only if you get your desired outcomes.

High achievers especially do this. Those who strive to succeed often feel the need to be continuously productive. They may have accomplished a remarkable amount, yet still feel an internal urge to do more in order to feel good about themselves. Such people become so focused on results that they lose track of their identity without them; thus, they spend all their time trying to obtain better and greater outcomes. If they don't meet their own criteria, they often berate themselves for it instead of seeking out healthier ways of coping. As such, they develop proficiency in one area (usually related to work), which can lead to an unbalanced lifestyle since they neglect their health or interpersonal relationships.

Are you following? Does this resonate with you?

CHAPTER 4 - WHAT IS THE EDEN MODEL?

Remember, this model is backwards. But it's the way most people go through it so it is helpful to understand.

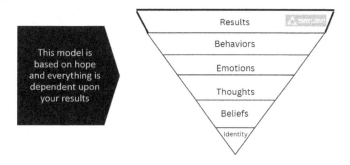

"I hope to get these results.

I hope this behavior works.

I hope I feel like it.

I hope that this makes sense.

I hope I believe in it

I hope I am good enough to do it."

Notice how the smallest section, Identity, is situated at the bottom of the model. Here, your identity is being called into question because it doesn't support your results. The model is so heavy on results that it seems to be crushing your entire sense of self. It is so easy to feel out of balance this way.

One more example

We all live in the world of social media and we all know how it feels when social media doesn't give us the results that we're looking for.

Have you ever made a post on social media and nobody liked or commented on it?

A flash of panic strikes in the pit of your stomach as you witness your post tumble into a dark, empty abyss. You feel invisible and without worth; chills run over your skin at the thought that nobody seems to care. Your mind races with questions: "Did I do something wrong? Does this mean I am not good enough?" Frantically, you double-check your settings to make sure it is set to Public, desperately clinging to the hope that somebody will still see it. But it's already too late - you've gone from longing for results straight to questioning your identity. It all comes crashing down on you with a force so powerful you can almost feel it.

The model does its thing—you go from results to identity in an instant. It's maddening how quickly your confidence fades away...

But what if the opposite happens?

Maybe you have one of those posts that just happens to go viral!

The thrill of success pulsates through you as your post goes viral! "Yes! I did this. Amazing!", you think. You start to believe that you can do anything, now armed with the knowledge and power of creating something viral. Suddenly, your identity screams at you: "I'm amazing! I made it." A wave of pride washes over you; this is who you are, a winner, a doer, someone amazing who can make things happen. The addictive effect of instant success is overwhelming; the results are tangible!

But this is unsustainable in the long run. As quickly as a celebrity singer's fame swells, it crashes when their fans move on to someone else.

Who are you independent of what your social media says?

***

If the triangle is upside down like this, it can stand for a while like a spinning top but that takes a lot of energy to keep it upright. The only sustainable option is to turn the model right side up like a pyramid and reverse the process.

The Model Correctly Applied

With a strong sense of identity, you have a solid foundation to build upon - which is the key to reaching your ultimate potential. Once this foundation is established, everything else will fall into place, leading you towards the results that you desire.

Let's break down this model and see how it works.

Knowing how important identity is, you may still ask, "But what about the results? Can't we start with the end of mind? Can't I have my goals? Can't I know what I'm looking for?"

Of course, you can! But the key is to keep your identity fixed and in mind when you're doing it.

Know who you are and believe in yourself first. That will keep you going.

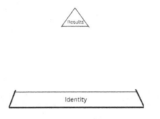

I want you to begin by asking yourself this question.

Who am I, independent of my results?

That is an important question. Why? Because many of my clients first come to me as high achievers: successful, driven, and have accomplished amazing things. Yet they say things like, "I don't know who I am without all this success." Or, "I am trying hard to reach the next level but it isn't working."

They have built up their sense of identity based on all their results. When they look at the rest of their life or start to see those results get shaky or overwhelming, their confidence is challenged. They feel out of balance in other areas of their life. Their relationships aren't fulfilling. Their health is suffering. They aren't having enough fun in their lives.

They don't know who they are outside of the results they have, because that's been their focus. They have been so good at it and that's why they keep doing it.

They have had times when they think, "I want to improve these other areas of my life, but I don't know how. It's uncomfortable. It's unusual... So I'm going to focus on what I'm good at, which happens to be my business."

And that is why people stay stuck.

Who are you, independent of your results?

This knowledge is crucial.

Understanding your worth and who you are independent of your results, allows you to recognize yourself as capable, strong, and deserving - qualities which will act as pillars of support throughout your journey to success.

You now have a strong foundation and can start to create steps on how to obtain those results in a sustainable and designed manner.

I want you to feel how this works.

What outcome are you currently trying to achieve?

More money? Growth? More time? More balance? Lose weight? More confidence?

Write it down at the top of your pyramid.

Let's say you chose to lose weight and feel more energetic.

Now, don't jump straight into creating a list of steps you must take to lose weight and feel more energetic. The burden of "how" may quickly become too much, and you might be tempted to quit before even beginning. It appears overwhelming because there is no base from which you can build up to see those results.

Here is where we go about the process differently in a way that will get you sustainable results.

> When you change what you see, everything you see changes. You first have to see it in your mind. This is the power of visualization.

Can you see yourself achieving your result? Can you identify with that result? Do you see yourself as worthy of it?

Rather than ask "What do I need to do to obtain this result?" ask, "How do I need to see myself in order to get this result?" In other words, "Who do I need to become to have this result?"

You can envision who you need to be and you can become that person now.

If you see yourself as capable, fit, confident, energetic, amazing, etc. you will act like it. When you have a new identity, or see yourself differently, everything else changes.

If you do this correctly you will begin to feel it in your heart and you'll start to make it real. If you don't, it'll just stay in your mind. Then it gets stuck and that's as far as it goes.

So let's say you see yourself as a fit, energetic, confident, and caring person who is able to spend time with those you love. You are confident in your body.

Now rephrase it to an "I am" statement and say it out loud to yourself until you feel it!

"I am fit, energetic, confident, and caring! I am confident in my body and I enjoy spending time with those I love!"

When you are able to see yourself for your true potential your beliefs are strong. You believe in yourself because you know it's possible. You've imagined it. You've seen it. Now you believe it.

Your envisioned future makes sense. Now you have a sense of certainty that you will get there.

A belief is a sense of certainty. You already know the results are going to come because you've already seen them. You already know that you're worthy and capable of losing weight and having the energy you want.

Because your belief and identity are strong, your thoughts are positive.

"Yes, I can lose weight and be more energetic! Yes, this is going to be worth it. Yes, I can do this. Yes, this is going to work!"

You create compelling stories of success to get you there, so when the inner critic starts to talk, you can respond with, "I already know who I am. I've already seen it. I'm just going to go create it."

You don't have to worry about all the nonsense that tries to convince you otherwise.

And because you have those powerful, positive thoughts, you don't have to wonder how you will feel today.

You have decided how you WANT to feel. You are excited, motivated, passionate, energetic, and ready to go!

Finally, you take action (implement the strategy) that gets you the results you want.

Because you have done it this way, you are ready to do whatever it takes to get the result you want. You are aligned. You feel amazing! You are so excited to do what you need to do to get the results that you want. Now you can do the workouts, meal plans, and whatever else you think will help you lose weight and gain more confidence because you know what they will do for you. You are already confident they will work.

You no longer see them as "I hope these work." You see them as "This is part of my design to get me my desired result."

Can you see the difference? Can you tell how that will make all the difference for intentional and sustainable results?

This keeps you focused and committed to your result.

This keeps you dedicated to and consistent with your behavior. You don't get discouraged by "failed" attempts. You see everything differently.

Because you have done it in this order, your results are much more achievable. You have started with a strong foundation - one that supports you and sustains you in your quest to achieve. You started by visualizing (seeing in your mind's eye) yourself achieving those results and now you see it happening in reality.

You designed it based on your identity, and everything now leads up to the results.

Is our sense of self really such a big deal?

Many times we don't realize that it is a limited sense of self that stops us from achieving. This is because it is uncommon for us to outright say to ourselves, "I just don't really see myself being successful at that. I am just not a (fill in the blank)." Although we don't say that outright, it is likely happening subconsciously.

For example, I was talking to a realtor who has been in his profession for 5 years. He now owns several properties and seems very confident in his plan to acquire more. He told me a story about one of his biggest regrets. He said that at the beginning of his career, someone offered him a triplex for a good deal. He chickened out and didn't take it. He now describes himself as having been young and stupid and truly regrets his decision.

He asked me what I coach people on so I told him I was writing a book and he asked what it was about. I asked him if I could answer that question by running his story through my model. He agreed.

I then asked him, "Did you know that all behavior is based on an emotional need?"

He responded skeptically, "What are you talking about?"

I said, "Yeah, think about it. Years ago, when you were considering buying the triplex, were you excited about it, or were you nervous about it?"

"Well, I was kind of nervous. I'd never done it before." He replied.

"OK, so you were nervous. And since you were nervous, did you think buying the triplex would make you feel better or worse?" I asked.

"I guess I thought it would make me feel worse and I didn't want to make a mistake," was his reply.

"Let me see if I understand," I said. "You were feeling uncomfortable, so you thought the best way to make yourself feel better would be to not buy the triplex. That way, you wouldn't have to continue experiencing those anxious feelings anymore. Does that sound right?"

"Yes, that does!" He said as it dawned on him what had happened.

Now, let's apply the model to this story and see what happened. He experienced all the steps of the model although he didn't realize what was going on at the time.

> *Result: He didn't get the triplex.*
> *Behavior: He chose not to buy.*
> *Emotion: Fear and uncertainty. Overwhelm. Anxiety.*
> *Thoughts: This is a bigger investment than I have ever made.*
> *Belief: The risk is too great on this. I am not ready.*
> *Identity: I am not a successful, confident realtor/investor right now.*

That was reality.

Here is how he saw the process:

> *Results: I don't have any properties.*
> *Behavior: I have listened to podcasts, read books, gone to meetings, looked at properties*
> *Emotion: I feel anxious and discouraged*
> *Thoughts: Why isn't this working? I am doing all the right things.*
> *Belief: Why is this so hard? I thought this would work.*
> *Identity: I guess I am not cut out to be a realtor.*

Here is what would happen if done correctly.

> *Identity: I am a successful realtor.*
> *Belief: I can do this! This is fun! I make smart decisions.*
> *Thoughts: Because I am working smart and hard, I will see success.*
> *Emotion: I am confident and optimistic.*
> *Behavior: I make my calls, visits, appointments, and commitments. I will take calculated risks.*
> *Results: I am buying and selling lots of properties!*

Do you see how this works? Using the Eden model and making sure your steps go in the right direction will lead to better and more lasting outcomes. Begin by understanding who you are, and it will guide you closer to achieving your goals instead of wishing for results that may or may not assuage your anxieties.

Are our beliefs really such a big deal?

Here's an example of how a client of mine had a belief that a certain result would solve his problems.

His dad committed suicide, his ex-wife continually threatened him with false charges, and his kids turned against him because of what his ex-wife told them - just to name a few things that were going on in his life.

He had a deep belief about money. He believed that "If I have enough money, it will fix everything else." He would not have to commit suicide like his dad did. He could show his ex-wife that he didn't need her. He could appear as a strong and successful father.

The problem with this thinking is that his fears are never satisfied with money. In other words, he will always think he has to have more money. It is never enough.

If this thinking continues, he will continue to experience anxiety because there is the constant fear of not having enough, losing what he has, and worrying about where more will come from.

We discovered this limiting belief and then reprogrammed it. The empowering belief he needed was "I am still loved because I have enough."

That is a more powerful mindset!

Seeing himself this way and having this belief allowed him to turn his negative thoughts into positive self-talk, helped him feel more excited and confident about his job, motivated him to put in the work, and ended up earning good money! The key here is that he didn't see the money as fixing problems. He saw it as a manifestation that he is and he has enough to be loved.

Because my client learned to see himself differently, he no longer needed so much external validation. He used to feel the need to buy the latest and greatest of everything. He would receive packages from Amazon almost daily. He has learned to see himself differently and now focuses on what is most important. He doesn't need these things anymore, saving him $1,000's a month.

Conclusion

You've seen how the model works and it makes sense. Now how can you use it for yourself?

You can catch yourself in each step of the model. Ask yourself, "Which part of the model am I in right now? Am I focused on my results?

Am I deciding on my behaviors? Am I in the midst of my emotions? Do I like what I am feeling?

What am I telling myself? What conversations am I having in my head? Do I like the stories I am telling myself? Or are they disempowering? What are my beliefs? What am I certain about? How do I see myself? How do I define myself? How do I label myself? And how do I see the world or this situation?"

Realizing where you are in the model allows you to ask yourself powerful questions that change how you see things.

Does the order matter?

In cognitive hierarchy, there is an order to things. People are emotional. If you want to influence someone, you must meet them at and influence their emotional state. This is the most effective way to get to their decision-making part of the brain - hence why storytelling is so powerful. This is the importance of leading with empathy.

If you want to have an impact on someone, start by establishing a connection. Rather than suggesting they change their behavior immediately, invite them out for something casual such as lunch, golf, or a meeting. If the person is comfortable with you emotionally, they will become more open to your ideas intellectually. When their beliefs align with yours and their identity is respected, things will begin to click in their mind and they will feel secure with you. The stronger the emotional bond between the two of you, the more likely it is that they will adhere to your suggestions when it comes to changing their behavior.

The cycle begins with where your focus is.

Order of operations. What are they doing? What are they feeling? What are they thinking? What do they believe? Who do they think they are?

In other words, is their behavior working? Do they feel safe? Do they feel heard? Do they feel understood? Do they believe in themselves and have a vision?

Ask yourself, "How can I see this differently?" If you struggle to answer that question, go up the model. You have to meet people where they are. Do something together. Acknowledge their emotions and let them process them. Talk it out.

Follow this model and you will get different results. It works because you are going about the process differently: identity, belief, mindset, and emotional processing. All before just choosing a new behavior.

If you are thinking, "This makes so much sense! I wonder why I have never seen it this way before" it is because there is one more complication to the model. Take a look below and I will explain.

How We Actually See the Model

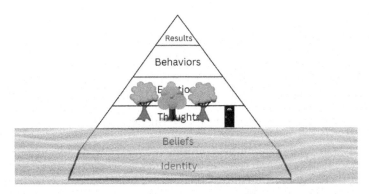

Now that you understand how the model works, let's go a little bit deeper. We will go to a level that coaches and other success professionals work in.

If you imagine the model as a pyramid in the sand, Beliefs and Identity are below the surface. They are in the subconscious - the part of the brain that is always at work, to your benefit or not. It takes help and effort to change your beliefs and identity.

Emotions and Thoughts can be seen if you care to get close enough. You know you have thoughts. You realize you have emotions. But it's kind of like seeing them through a bunch of trees - or a forest depending on your familiarity. Sometimes you don't understand your emotions. You just want to watch TV or distract yourself because you don't want to deal with them.

And your thoughts? You are stuck in your thoughts all the time, aren't you? Sometimes you don't know you have power over them and you don't know what to do otherwise. You repeatedly think negative thoughts and end up believing them!

It takes practice to observe your own thoughts and emotions.

Because of the ground and all the trees, all we see of this model are the results and behaviors. This explains why these are most often discussed in books, trainings, seminars, etc.

That's why we all act this way—we believe that if you want the outcome to be different, you have to do something different. It should be that easy, right? So why isn't it?

Are you beginning to realize that there is more than meets the eye when it comes to what drives our behaviors?

The door to change

The more you learn about the model and how it works, the more you can alter your perspective as you observe and reprogram it to meet your needs rather than just being a passive participant and hoping the outcome is favorable.

The good news is that you do have the power to change how you experience the model. Notice that there is a door on the pyramid. A door to your thoughts.

The only influence we have is through the doorway to thought. This is where most people get stuck. It is also where the most influence for change happens. It is the opening for how you can change each section of the model.

This is where you tell yourself stories and have conversations with yourself. It is where you weigh the pros and cons and assign meaning to a situation.

This is where you contemplate; where you "understand it intellectually or conceptually."

Since this is where most people get stuck, this is where most people are familiar. This is where anxiety is stirred up. It is where confidence is born.

You may not be able to control what happens in your life but you can control your mind.

Every part of the model is affected by your thoughts. You pass judgment on each section.

You focus on it, decide if you like what you see or not, and then feel either content or dissatisfied. If you are content, you carry on with the same approach. If you are not, you feel dissatisfied and seek out another option.

Thoughts, emotions, and actions are all closely related and can influence each other in various ways. Here's a brief explanation of how they are related:

Thoughts and Emotions: Our thoughts can trigger emotions, and our emotions can affect our thoughts. For example, if we have negative thoughts about a situation, we may feel anxious or sad. On the other hand, if we have positive thoughts, we may feel happy or hopeful. In this way, our thoughts and emotions can influence each other in a continuous feedback loop. If we don't know why we feel a certain way, our brain comes up with ideas to justify why we feel that way - which is why you blame someone else for something even when it wasn't their fault.

Thoughts and Actions: Our thoughts can also influence our actions. If we have positive thoughts about a situation, we may be more likely to take action and pursue our goals. Conversely, negative thoughts may lead us to avoid taking action or give up on our goals. Our thoughts can also affect the quality of our actions, as they can impact our motivation, focus, and confidence.

Emotions and Actions: Our emotions can also influence our actions. If we are feeling anxious or stressed, we may be more likely to procrastinate or avoid tasks. Conversely, if we are feeling motivated or inspired, we may be more likely to take action and achieve our goals. Our emotions can also affect the quality of our actions, as they can impact our energy, creativity, and problem-solving abilities.

Thoughts, emotions, and actions are all interconnected and can influence each other in various ways. By understanding the relationship between these three elements, we can develop strategies to manage our thoughts and emotions and take action toward achieving our goals.

Summary

If I can influence your thoughts, then I can help you look at things in a different light. By providing mental guidance, I can expand both sides of your thought process. Not only can I alter how you feel, but ultimately help redefine how you see yourself.

You can learn to do this for yourself as well. It all starts with your inner voice. This is the reason why having a positive mindset is so crucial - it is the access point and influences everything else.

Here is where I could give you a comprehensive list of things you can do to improve your mindset. I could tell you to implement all these things and your life will be completely different!

I'm not denying the benefits of lists. However, I am saying that if you just focus on new behaviors, it won't provide anything more than a temporary fix. It can offer a glimmer of hope, but if it doesn't work, everything looks like a failure - including you.

"But I want the list! I want the steps that tell me what to do."

You can go anywhere you want and get a list of things to do. ChatGpt can give you easy lists. You could ask the latest influencers for their opinion.

I know many other people give lists, but if I can get you to go to a level deeper than behavior, you will get more sustainable results.

With the Eden model and new way of thinking, you get to decide and understand why a certain behavior would work for you. You won't just pick something random off the list and hope it works.

With whatever behavior you choose, the Eden model will help you do it and get good at it until it becomes natural. It becomes a part of you.

If you can go deep enough, with the right help, and do it in the right way, you begin to transform and things start to work not by chance, but by design.

Here's the great news! You are already following this model. You don't have to learn anything new. You just have to make modifications to what you are currently doing.

You can apply this model and have better results every time. What it does is dissect what is happening, helps you understand how the brain works, and allows you to reprogram the process.

An additional perspective

You have read this far because you're tired of feeling frustrated, a lack of control, and anxious. You are tired of feeling those emotions and not knowing what to do about them. You are tired of being stuck in your mind, hoping results come but you feel like nothing is working. You are driven, capable, motivated, and ready to build the business and lifestyle of your dreams.

You can go through this model yourself and make good progress. You can even tell people that you are doing this. In fact, research studies have shown that publicly committing your goals to someone gives you at least a 65% chance of completing them. However, having a specific accountability partner, whether it is God, a coach, or someone else, increases your chance of success to 95%.

That's amazing! Who wouldn't want that kind of certainty of success?

It helps to have an outside perspective from somebody who sees you for who you truly are.

Sometimes we forget who we truly are, don't we?

Sometimes we look in the mirror and wonder, who is that?

You think you are a loser. You are never going to make this work. You see the negative and you get stuck there.

So reach out to someone who can give you that empowering outside perspective. Reach out to God. He knows you better than anyone. He knows your true potential and can help you get there. Talk to a coach. Find an accountability partner who sees you for who you truly are and believes in you completely. Find someone who will say to you, "You are amazing. You are totally capable of doing this. Look at all the things that are working!"

This outside view can help remind you of your identity, help you see and change your limiting beliefs, change your thoughts, master emotions, try new things, and get different results.

It requires you to step out of the pyramid (get out of your head) and get a new perspective.

Who will you ask to be your accountability partner?

Summary of Chapter 4

- A strong sense of identity provides a solid foundation for personal growth and success.

- Identifying oneself beyond external results is crucial for maintaining balance and fulfillment.

- Visualizing and believing in one's potential leads to a sense of certainty, positive thoughts, and aligned actions towards achieving desired outcomes.

Questions for Application:

- Who are you, independent of your current results or achievements?

- Can you vividly visualize yourself attaining your desired outcome? Do you believe in this vision?

- How can you rephrase your envisioned future into a powerful "I am" statement to reinforce your belief in your potential?

- Who will you ask to be your accountability partner as you create this envisioned future?

Part 2

The remaining pages of the book will dive deeper into each section of the Eden model so you can work through it yourself. You can read these in order or you can turn to a particular section to learn more to meet your needs.

Chapter 5 - Identity: How Do You See Yourself?

How you see yourself, the world, a situation.

How you define or label yourself.

Your self concept

The role you play

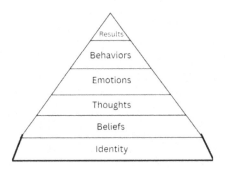

O n Christmas Eve 1914, in the dank, muddy trenches on the Western Front of the first world war, a remarkable thing happened.

It came to be called the Christmas Truce. And it remains one of the most storied and strangest moments of the Great War—or of any war in history.

British machine gunner Bruce Bairnsfather, later a prominent cartoonist, wrote about it in his memoirs. Like most of his fellow infantrymen of the 1st Battalion of the Royal Warwickshire Regiment, he was spending the holiday eve shivering in the muck, trying to keep warm. He had spent a good part of the past few months fighting the Germans. And now, in a part of Belgium called Bois de Ploegsteert, he was crouched in a trench that stretched just three feet deep by three feet wide, his days and nights marked by an endless cycle of sleeplessness and fear, stale biscuits and cigarettes too wet to light.

"Here I was, in this horrible clay cavity," Bairnsfather wrote, "...miles and miles from home. Cold, wet through and covered with mud." There didn't "seem the slightest chance of leaving—except in an ambulance."

At about 10 p.m., Bairnsfather noticed a noise. "I listened," he recalled. "Away across the field, among the dark shadows beyond, I could hear the murmur of voices." He turned to a fellow soldier in his trench and said, "Do you hear the Boches [Germans] kicking up that racket over there?"

"Yes," came the reply. "They've been at it some time!"

The Germans were singing carols, as it was Christmas Eve. In the darkness, some of the British soldiers began to sing back. "Suddenly," Bairnsfather recalled, "we heard a confused shouting from the other side. We all stopped to listen. The shout came again." The voice was from an enemy soldier, speaking in English with a strong German accent. He was saying, "Come over here."

One of the British sergeants answered: "You come half-way. I come half-way."

What happened next would, in the years to come, stun the world and make history. Enemy soldiers began to climb nervously out of their trenches, and to meet in the barbed-wire-filled "No Man's Land" that separated the armies. Normally, the British and Germans communicated across No Man's Land with streaking bullets, with only occasional gentlemanly allowances to collect the dead unmolested. But now, there were handshakes and words of kindness. The soldiers traded songs, tobacco and wine, joining in a spontaneous holiday party in the cold night.

Bairnsfather could not believe his eyes. "Here they were—the actual, practical soldiers of the German army. There was not an atom of hate on either side."

The moment the two sides decided to see themselves and each other not as enemies but as human beings just trying to celebrate Christmas, they were able to put aside their weapons (hurtful thoughts, words, and weapons) and spend peaceful time together.

Not Everyone Was Pleased With the Truce

In another account, a German scolded his fellow soldiers during the Christmas Truce: "Such a thing should not happen in wartime. Have you no German sense of honor left?" That 25-year old soldier's name was Adolf Hitler."

Hitler's sense of self was such that he thought pure Germans were better than everyone else and that the land needed to be purified. He did horrendous things because of how he saw himself and the world. That just illustrates the power of an identity.

Our sense of identity, which is the way we see ourselves, can have a significant impact on how we behave in various situations. Here are a few ways that our sense of identity can affect our behavior:

1. If we see ourselves as confident, competent, and capable, we are more likely to behave in ways that reflect those qualities. On the other hand, if we see ourselves as insecure, inadequate, or flawed, we may be more likely to avoid challenges, doubt ourselves, or give up easily.

    a. Your sense of identity is composed of your beliefs and perceptions about yourself, as well as how you view the world. Your self-esteem encompasses your feelings about yourself, while your self-knowledge covers what you know about yourself. Your social self reflects how you show up with other people.

2. Values and Beliefs: Our sense of identity is also influenced by our values and beliefs, which are the principles and ideas that we hold to be important and true. Our values and beliefs can shape our behavior by guiding our decisions, actions, and priorities. For example, if we value honesty and integrity, we are more likely to behave honestly and ethically, even in difficult situations.

3. Social Identity: Our sense of identity is also influenced by our social identity, or the groups that we belong to and the roles we play within those groups. Our social identity can affect our behavior by shaping our attitudes, beliefs, and behaviors towards others who belong to the same or different groups. If we identify strongly with a particular political or social group, we may be more likely to adopt their beliefs and behaviors.

For example, if you want to be a leader, you will seek to identify yourself as a leader. To fit in as a leader you will do what is necessary to qualify to be seen as a leader. You will prepare for meetings, you will look a certain way, you will act a certain way. You may even give in to social influence because that is what certain leaders do.

Religion is one of the clearest examples of how we see ourselves and how this model works. If you identify as a Christian and your friend identifies as a Muslim, you automatically have different beliefs, which influence your thoughts, emotions, behaviors, and results. If you see each other for your differences, you will have conflict. If you see each other for what you have in common (ie. identity as a fellow human being), you will build bridges of understanding.

Overall, our sense of identity can affect how we perceive ourselves and others, how we make decisions, and how we behave in various situations. By understanding the impact of our identity on our behavior, we can work to develop a positive and authentic sense of self, align our values and beliefs with our actions, and cultivate healthy relationships with others.

Identity in Sports

Walt Disney Pictures released a sports drama film in 2006 called "Invincible." It is based on the true story of Vince Papale, a bartender and part-time substitute teacher from Philadelphia, who fulfills his dream of playing for the National Football League (NFL).

In the summer of 1976, 30-year-old Vince Papale was having a tough run of luck. He was working as a substitute teacher for two days a week but found out that his job had been eliminated because of budget cuts. His wife gave up on him saying he would never amount to anything and asked for a divorce. He worked as a part-time bartender and played football with his friends. When the new coach of the Philadelphia Eagles, Dick Vermeil, announced that he would hold open tryouts for the team, Vince reluctantly decided to give it a try.

Papale loved football but never thought he would play for the NFL. He was told in high school that he was too small to play football!

Papale had to conquer both how others saw him and how he saw himself. Others thought he was too old. He thought he wasn't good enough. He had lost his part-time job, his wife gave up on him, and he was raised being told he couldn't make it because he was too small.

Throughout the movie, you start to see how he begins to see himself differently and believe in himself. If he didn't see that, he would have given up after a few practices. But against all odds, Papale managed to impress the coaching staff and earned a spot on the team, becoming the oldest rookie in NFL history. As he struggled to prove himself to his skeptical teammates and the fans, Vince's determination and hard work inspired both his fellow players and the city of Philadelphia.

That is a story of individual identity. Now let's see how everyone's sense of identity affects things.

In the middle of the movie, a new bartender shows up amongst all these Eagles fans. The new bartender is a die-hard Giants fan. Before they knew anything else about each other, they judged each other. All they could see were Giants fans vs Eagles fans.

Now see what happens here.

They watch the same game! Everything that happens on the field is the same for each fan but the interpretation is extremely different so their experience of the game is not similar at all. If the Giants score, the Giants fans are happy while the Eagles are upset. If both fans are sitting next to each other, this can cause some contention. Each thinks of the other, "Because you cheer for the other team (behavior), I see you as an enemy (identity). I am upset when you are happy. Your team better not win."

Because your identity is different, your thoughts, emotions, and behavior are different, getting you different results.

This principle is even more apparent when two friends can cheer for opposite teams. During the game, the friends may despise each other and may even fight a little. But after the game, if they can go back to being friends, then what they have done shows how changing how they see themselves (opposite fans vs best friends) can change everything else about their relationship.

This is a common occurrence in many aspects of daily life: religion, politics, sports, cliques, schools, work, etc. If you identify with a certain group, and if you feel strongly enough about a different group, you will judge those people in the other group as very different from you and possibly even your enemy.

How we see others

IDENTITY

Here is where another view of the Eden Model comes in.

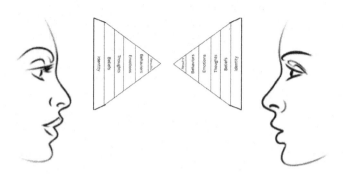

Every day, we each look through the model as our lens. When we look at someone else, we see their results and judge them based on their behavior. We then skip the rest of the model to judge their identity.

"I can't believe they broke the plate (result and behavior)! What an idiot (identity)."

"That bozo (identity) cut me off (behavior)!"

We quickly jump to judging someone else's identity.

We don't do that to ourselves though.

> "We judge ourselves by our intentions and others by their behavior." - Stephen Covey

When we think of our own actions, we focus on our intentions: was it meant to offend anyone? With others, however, we judge solely by their behavior. We observe whether it is "good" or "bad" and form an opinion of them without thinking of the emotions, thoughts, and sense of self that led to this behavior.

If we made more of an effort to understand these underlying causes in both ourselves and others, there would be more empathy in the world today. Then we would show more compassion and be able to make the desired changes in the world.

How we see ourselves affects how we see others.

Naming vs Labeling

Have you ever taken a personality test and received your results? It is fascinating to see which type of behaviors fits your personality and how it can help you understand why you do what you do. It's like finding an identity that you can connect with; it's as if you suddenly have things in common with people who share the same "identity" as you. Your language changes, too--you start saying things like, "That's definitely me!" or "That's not really me."

While these tests can be fun and helpful, I would caution you not to label yourself solely by these results. Those who do end up looking for ways to live up to that label or justify everything they do by that label.

Identity is the real name of something. Labeling is attaching a belief (associating a meaning) to that identity. You can put a label around chicken and call it beef but it is still chicken.

This can work in disempowering and empowering ways.

Let's suppose you have wondered why you struggle to put yourself out there in social situations. You want to talk to more people and build more relationships but you are overwhelmed with the fear of what they will say or what they will think. You finally discover that this is called anxiety.

You now have two choices.

You can say (label), "I have anxiety" or, "I am an anxious person."

OR

You can say (name), "I experience anxiety." or "I feel anxious when I think of talking to people."

Do you feel the difference? There is a different feeling when you name a behavior or emotion vs when you label yourself.

Now let's consider you just discovered a strength of yours. Maybe you have high emotional intelligence and you score high in empathy. "Empathy" is the name of your strength. "Empath" or "empathetic" is a label for you.

Say this out loud and see how it feels different.

"I scored high in empathy. Empathy is my strength."

Now say, "I am empathetic. I am an Empath."

Again, say these out loud and feel the difference!

The naming of something is always empowering. Why? Because it clarifies a previously unknown experience into something that is separate from you. It doesn't limit you because it doesn't define you. It is simply something you experience from time to time. You can change a label into a behavior by changing "I am a pessimist" into "Sometimes I have a tendency to act in pessimistic ways."

Many people use labels to describe their identity. If you insist on using labels, make sure you use empowering titles.

One way to test if a label is empowering or disempowering is to observe what you believe, think, feel, and do with that label. What results do you get if you accept that label?

If I say my baby is an "easy" baby, I won't mind when he has an occasional hard night because I am grateful he is such an easy baby. But if I say he is a "hard" baby and he has ANOTHER hard night, I will probably be frustrated. The same thing happened but my experience was different because I saw my baby differently.

If you say kids are dumb or the weather is stupid, guess how you will feel about them?

This is why I don't like labels. Labels are so limiting. They attempt to define someone's identity and they usually fall short.

Labels are for tin cans, so don't label yourself.

Growing into your identity

You have seen how the Eden model can work in both directions. You can change your behavior, work on emotions, change your story, change your beliefs, and your sense of self changes. Or it can be done by imagining what type of person you want to be and asking yourself, "How would that person be spiritually, mentally, physically, emotionally, etc.?" You clarify that in your mind and on paper and then start to make progress to get there. What would that person have to believe? What stories would that person tell themselves? How would they feel on a regular basis? How would they act? What results would they get? Then take steps to make that person you.

We often grow into our identity. Kids grow into it through their teenage years. They grow physically and develop mentally while discovering who they want to be.

Every good story is about someone changing and growing into their identity. The victim becomes the victor. Frodo becomes the hero. Harry Potter goes from the Boy Who Lived to the Wizard Who Took

Down Voldemort. Rocky went from a nobody to a champion. When Simon became Peter, he had a new identity and acted differently. It took him some time to change that identity. The same happened when Saul became Paul.

How we feel about how we see ourselves

I was at the chiropractor and my doctor hadn't received his license yet so he could only do limited treatments and most people referred to him by his first or last name. Finally, on the day his license arrived in the mail, his boss called him "Doc." It was as if I could sense the pride in the room as this new doctor heard his title being used. He saw himself in a much better light because he attached so much meaning to that identity.

I spoke to a leader who knew they wanted to grow their company and needed to bring in more sales to do so. Her team of salespeople wasn't bringing in the business needed.

They had two choices. Build or buy. Do they find new salespeople (buy) or do they try to elevate the performance of those they have (build)?

You have to consider opportunity cost here (time to train, cost to train, and if you have the right people on the bus vs time and cost to buy and hope you get the right people on the bus).

How do you build and elevate your people?

I am not talking about threats or rewards here. I am talking about understanding your people, building trust with them, and enabling them to reach their ultimate potential. Doing so will get you better long-term results because you access the power of their mind as well instead of just relying on yours alone.

Let's apply the Eden Model here. You want more sales (result). Do you find a new behavior (script)? Do you hype them up as they show up to the calls (emotion)? Do you help them get in the right state of mind (thoughts/mindset)? Do you help them believe in themselves and help them discover a powerful reason to succeed? Do they even see themselves as salespeople?

Before you buy a new strategy (behavior) check people's emotions and mindset. If they are scared and don't believe it is possible, no strategy is going to fix it for them. If you do happen to find the perfect strategy that works you may convince people for a while, but their confidence will be in the strategy and not in themselves. Their confidence will last only as long as the strategy does.

As we talked, the leader revealed that the salespeople she had were fresh out of college and had gotten this position in hopes of growing into different positions later. None of them had a passion for sales. None of them saw themselves in the position for much longer.

No wonder they weren't bringing in the sales needed! In this case, they didn't see themselves as salespeople and therefore didn't perform in the role.

***

The reason powerful speakers are so successful is because they can get to the depth of what I'm talking about here. They can help you see yourself and see the world differently. As you do so your beliefs and thoughts change, your emotions change, your behavior changes and you get different results. So why do so many people not understand this? Why do people still focus so heavily on just changing behavior?

It's probably because behavior drives results. People want results. Results earn money. Results bring desired change.

In business, people want a different result. Great! Let's say you want to get more customers (result). So the behavior change is that you want to have people buy. But if you just focus on behavior and want people to buy then what will you do? You will probably try to convince them and give them some incentive. You may spend more money on marketing or hire more salespeople. You might give discounts or coupons. You might spend more time at networking events. But if your customers don't have the right thoughts or emotions regarding your product they will not buy.

Remember how people make emotional decisions? Buying is an emotional decision rationalized by logic. What does this mean? It means people buy because they feel like it. They feel good about it and they have found a way that makes sense in their mind. So how do you make this happen?

If you want people to act differently, you must not only give them a new, compelling idea, but you must give them something to identify with. You have to influence how they see themselves and link your product to that identity. People unite under a common identity. Eagles fan. Student. Entrepreneur. Leader. Parent.

Cotopaxi sells outdoor gear. If Cotopaxi simply told their customers that they are buying outdoor gear with great material and bright colors, they might convince a few to buy. But they won't have raving, long-term customers.

Cotopaxi does more than sell outdoor products. Part of their logo is "Gear for Good." Their mission statement is: "We create outdoor products and experiences that help alleviate poverty, move people to do good, and inspire adventure."

People align with their vision of alleviating poverty.

Before Cotopaxi even began selling outdoor products, they hosted "Questivals." The idea was to make discovering the great outdoors a fun experience. The participants in the first Questival painted the Cotopaxi logo onto their own bags, hats, and clothing - they even spray-painted their cars! People loved the event and the mission to fight poverty so much that they wanted to identify with it.

Because they told their customers a story that influenced the way they saw themselves and the way they saw the world they got much different results.

The CEO had done some personal research and realized there was a trend among young people to support companies that have ethics they can relate to and to choose brands that do good for the environment and society. He capitalized on this finding and now has thousands of people who identify with his brand and mission.

If your customers see that your product helps them feel better about themselves or helps them feel better about the world then they will buy your product. You help them understand that someone who buys Cotopaxi gear is someone who is helping to alleviate poverty. Not only that, but they are responsible and fit and enjoy the outdoors. This is why ads contain pictures of people they want to be like. They identify with these people.

You have influenced their beliefs and thoughts and they now feel, by purchasing the outdoor gear, like they are becoming part of making the world a better place. They see themselves differently, they see their place in this world differently, and they see the world differently because they believe that their thoughts of "How can I do this? What should I buy?" make them feel good and make them feel motivated to buy this clothing. If you can link status to something, people will see beyond the price tag and even pay top dollar for it.

IDENTITY

And so you see that this works in business. If you can influence self-concept (identity) and beliefs you will get people to change their behavior and get the results you want.

***

If your results align with how you see yourself, you feel good about them. If the results go against your identity you feel guilt and shame.

In the Disney movie, Mulan, the main character returns home from a humiliating and failed attempt to impress her matchmaker. Because of this epic mistake, she questions her identity. "How could I have been so stupid? I am such an idiot! I am not cut out for this." (When something goes wrong, we all do this, don't we?)

She knows her actions are not aligned with how she sees herself.

She sings a song that expresses how she feels about wanting to show the world who she really is instead of pretending to be who she is not, but is afraid to disappoint her family by doing so.

"Look at me

I will never pass for a perfect bride

Or a perfect daughter

Can it be

I'm not meant to play this part

Now I see, that if I were truly to be myself

I would break my family's heart

Who is that girl I see

Staring straight back at me

Why is my reflection someone I don't know

Somehow I cannot hide

Who I am, though I've tried

When will my reflection show who I am inside

Mulan eventually ended up doing what she felt was right and made her family proud.

There was a man who would say "I'm starting a journal." He would struggle to be consistent and would feel terrible about himself. It wasn't until he decided to change his identity by choosing to say "I am a journal writer" that suddenly he was able to be consistent. That consistency came because he knew he needed to do the work to make the identity change real, i.e."If I'm a daily journal writer, then I need to make sure I am doing it daily, including today."

We all have an ideal self in our minds. Use it as motivation. You can either believe in that ideal self or you can judge yourself against it. One helps you grow. The other discourages you. The key is to see it as an aspiration or something you are working towards. Not something that has to happen today. Make your 1% improvement every day and eventually, you will get there.

Change your mindset. Instead of thinking, "I am not there yet. I keep making mistakes. I am untrue to my ideal self. I will never get there." You can change it to, "I am strong, capable, kind, loving, patient, and understanding. I am making progress every day and growing into the person I know I can become."

What is the identity you feed every day?

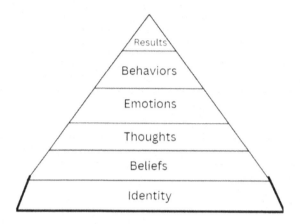

Conclusion

Look at the model. What part do you focus on? Which section do you use to define yourself?

If you use any section besides Identity, you will seek outside validation to help you feel better about yourself. This is something we inherently learn throughout our life - from living with our parents, to school, work, etc. "Do they think I am doing a good job?" If so, I have inner confidence. If not, I might struggle with my confidence. But if you can know your personal values - who you are and what is important to you - you will find internal validation everywhere you go and not have to rely on others' opinions of you.

The deep thought of an identity is "That's just how I am." So who are you? What do you want? What will you do about it?

The more you grow, the more sure of yourself you become. This is the power of masterminds. The fastest way to grow is to surround yourself with people who inspire you - those who have already grown to where you want to grow.

Are you an Implementor? An Ideator? A Visionary? You can't be more than one at a time - at least not if you want it to be sustainable.

Often, entrepreneurs and leaders are Visionaries, but if they want to grow, they have to hire out work as soon as possible. They can't be Implementors as well. In other words, they can't come up with all the ideas and make the ideas at the same time.

The Implementors may look at the Visionaries and judge saying, "We do all the work! You do nothing but play around and go to extravagant meetings!" But the Visionary is doing what they do best. Something the Implementor is not in a place to do. And the Implementor is providing tremendous value in making the Visionary's vision a reality.

Patrick Lencioni's "Working Genius" explains why this works. We have areas of Genius and areas of Frustration. We have roles that we better identify with because of our Geniuses. The more we can work in those areas, the longer we can sustain what we do.

Summary of Chapter 5

- Our sense of identity, shaped by our beliefs, values, and social affiliations, profoundly influences our behavior, decisions, and interactions with others.

- There is a difference between naming (neutral identification of behaviors or experiences) and labeling (attaching value judgments or beliefs to an identity). Use empowering titles rather than limiting labels.

- Individuals often grow into their identities, like children's development and the protagonist's transformation in stories. Engage in thought self-reflection and visualization to positively shape your identity.

Questions:

- How do you see yourself? How do you define your identity? Are there any labels you use that may be limiting your potential?

- Can you recall a time when a shift in your identity positively impacted your behavior or outcomes? What led to that change?

- In what areas of your life do you feel aligned with your ideal self? How can you nurture and reinforce this sense of identity to further your personal growth and success?

- How can your accountability partner help you with this?

Chapter 6 - Belief: What Do You Believe About Yourself?

A belief is a feeling of certainty.

A thought fused with emotion.

> *"Until I see myself differently, I will just copy your behavior to try and fit in."*

Let's review the classic story of "The Emperor's New Clothes" by Hans Christian Anderson. I will include the story here and make commentary to illustrate what parts of the model are being applied.

Many years ago there was an Emperor so exceedingly fond of new clothes that he spent all his money on being well dressed. He cared nothing about reviewing his soldiers, going to the theatre, or going for a ride in his carriage, except to show off his new clothes. He had a coat for every hour of the day, and instead of saying, as one might, about any other ruler, "The King's in council," here they always said. "The Emperor's in his dressing room."

In the great city where he lived, life was always gay. Every day many strangers came to town, and among them one day came two swindlers. They let it be known they were weavers (identity - they told people this is how they should see them), *and they said they could weave the most magnificent fabrics imaginable. Not only were their colors and patterns uncommonly fine, but clothes made of this cloth had a wonderful way of becoming invisible to anyone who was unfit for his office, or who was unusually stupid.* (belief)

"Those would be just the clothes for me," thought the Emperor. "If I wore them I would be able to discover which men in my empire are unfit for their posts. And I could tell the wise men from the fools. (Thoughts - the story he told himself) *Yes, I certainly* (strong emotion/belief) *must get some of the stuff woven for me right away." He paid the two swindlers a large sum of money* (behavior) *to start work at once.*

They set up two looms and pretended to weave, though there was nothing on the looms. All the finest silk and the purest old thread which they demanded went into their traveling bags, while they worked the empty looms far into the night.

"I'd like to know how those weavers are getting on with the cloth," the Emperor thought, (he wanted to have positive justification for his behavior by checking on the results) *but he felt slightly uncomfortable when he remembered that those who were unfit for their position would not be able to see the fabric. It couldn't have been that he doubted himself, yet he thought he'd rather send someone else to see how things were going. The whole town knew about the cloth's peculiar power, and all were impatient to find out how stupid their neighbors were.* (Everyone is caught up in this false belief and it affects all their thoughts and conversations)

"I'll send my honest old minister to the weavers," the Emperor decided. *"He'll be the best one to tell me how the material looks, for he's a sensible man and no one does his duty better."* (Now he is trying to solve his dilemma with a new behavior)

So the honest old minister went to the room where the two swindlers (notice how Anderson switches which identity he uses through the story - he helps us remember the truth while also seeing it from their perspective) *sat working away at their empty looms.*

"Heaven help me," he thought as his eyes flew wide open, *"I can't see anything at all". But he did not say so.*

Both the swindlers begged (strong behavior affecting his emotions) *him to be so kind* (teasing his true sense of self - his values) *as to come near to approve the excellent pattern, the beautiful colors. They pointed to the empty looms, and the poor old minister stared as hard as he dared. He couldn't see anything, because there was nothing to see.* (He saw the truth but he rationalized it away because of his tainted belief) *"Heaven have mercy,"* he thought. *"Can it be that I'm a fool? I'd have never guessed it, and not a soul must know. Am I unfit to be the minister? It would never do to let on that I can't see the cloth."* (When we have done something that goes against our values, we are tempted to hide it)

"Don't hesitate to tell us what you think of it," said one of the weavers. (Anderson is reminding us that the minister believes they are weavers and not swindlers)

"Oh, it's beautiful -it's enchanting." The old minister peered through his spectacles. *"Such a pattern, what colors!" I'll be sure to tell the Emperor how delighted I am with it."* (He thinks his behavior will get him the results he wants)

"We're pleased to hear that," the swindlers said. *They proceeded to name all the colors and to explain the intricate pattern.* (They exaggerate the story to be even more convincing. This is where we must be extra careful. Our stories can deceive us if we let them.) *The old minister paid the closest attention, so that he could tell it all to the Emperor. And so he did.*

The swindlers at once asked for more money, more silk and gold thread, to get on with the weaving. (The minister is so deep in his story and emotions - needing to be seen as reputable and not a fool - that he is willing to go to extreme behavior to try to justify what is happening). *But it all went into their pockets. Not a thread went into the looms, though they worked at their weaving as hard as ever.*

The Emperor presently sent another trustworthy official to see how the work progressed and how soon it would be ready. The same thing happened to him that had happened to the minister. He looked and he looked, but as there was nothing to see in the looms he couldn't see anything. (As we read this story, we are not as emotionally invested as these characters are. Thus we can see the truth for what it is. These characters see the truth as well - it isn't hidden from them - but they rationalize it away because they feel pressured not to look unfit for their office or unusually stupid (identity).

"Isn't it a beautiful piece of goods?" the swindlers asked him, as they displayed and described their imaginary pattern. (Here is the Cue)

"I know I'm not stupid," the man thought, "so it must be that I'm unworthy of my good office. (Isn't it interesting how we can take two false beliefs and strengthen our belief in one by the process of elimination?) *That's strange. I mustn't let anyone find it out, though."* (Their emotional need, or Craving, is to appear fit for their position - to feel good enough. So they choose a behavior they think, based on their beliefs and stories, will get them that result - even if it goes against their values). *So he praised the material he did not see. He declared he was delighted with the beautiful colors and the exquisite pattern.* (Response – He lied) *To the Emperor he said, "It held me spellbound."* (Perhaps he is grappling with his inner honesty. He knows what he saw - or didn't see-, but doesn't want to be seen as not good enough, so he tells a white lie to feel better about it. – Reward)

All the town was talking of this splendid cloth (peoples' stories are getting out of hand), *and the Emperor wanted to see it for himself while it was still in the looms. Attended by a band of chosen men, among whom were his two old trusted officials-the ones who had been to the weavers-he set out to see the two swindlers. He found them weaving with might and main, but without a thread in their looms.*

"Magnificent," said the two officials already duped. "Just look, Your Majesty, what colors! What a design!" They pointed to the empty looms, each supposing that the others could see the stuff. (Now the pressure is on because not only is the whole town talking about it, but once again, the Emperor is being reminded of the false belief by his two trusted officials! Notice that the swindlers didn't even have to say anything this time.)

"What's this?" thought the Emperor. "I can't see anything. This is terrible!

Am I a fool? Am I unfit to be the Emperor? What a thing to happen to me of all people! - (Here is a powerful thing to notice. Every time someone is face to face with the truth, they have a conversation in their mind. This is where they can decide to tell the truth or rationalize it away. This is where our power lies.) *Oh! It's very pretty," he said. "It has my highest approval." And he nodded approbation at the empty loom. Nothing could make him say that he couldn't see anything.* (Now he is so caught up in the belief; which this was all based on how he saw himself in the first place - as someone who was only good enough if he had the right clothes on.)

His whole retinue stared and stared. One saw no more than another, but (because they all thought there must be something they could not see) *they all joined the Emperor in exclaiming, "Oh! It's very pretty," and they advised him to wear clothes made of this wonderful cloth especially for the great procession he was soon to lead. "Magnificent! Excellent! Unsurpassed!"* (strong emotional words) *were bandied from mouth to mouth, and everyone did his best to seem well pleased. The Emperor gave each of the swindlers a cross to wear in his buttonhole, and the title of "Sir Weaver."* (They had convinced him of a false identity so he would believe them.)

Before the procession the swindlers sat up all night and burned more than six candles, to show how busy they were finishing the Emperor's new clothes. They pretended to take the cloth off the loom. They made cuts in the air with huge scissors. (All this extravagant behavior to try to cover their false identity) *And at last they said, "Now the Emperor's new clothes are ready for him."*

Then the Emperor himself came with his noblest noblemen, and the swindlers each raised an arm as if they were holding something. They said, "These are the trousers, here's the coat, and this is the mantle," naming each garment. "All of them are as light as a spider web. One would almost think he had nothing on, but that's what makes them so fine."

"Exactly," all the noblemen agreed, though they could see nothing, for there was nothing to see.

"If Your Imperial Majesty will condescend to take your clothes off," said the swindlers, "we will help you on with your new ones here in front of the long mirror."

The Emperor undressed, and the swindlers pretended to put his new clothes on him, one garment after another. They took him around the waist and seemed to be fastening something - that was his train-as the Emperor turned round and round before the looking glass.

"How well Your Majesty's new clothes look. Aren't they becoming!" He heard on all sides, "That pattern, so perfect! Those colors, so suitable! It is a magnificent outfit."

Then the minister of public processions announced: "Your Majesty's canopy is waiting outside."

"Well, I'm supposed to be ready," the Emperor said, and turned again for one last look in the mirror. "It is a remarkable fit, isn't it?" He seemed to regard his costume with the greatest interest.

The noblemen who were to carry his train stooped low and reached for the floor as if they were picking up his mantle. Then they pretended to lift and hold it high. They didn't dare admit they had nothing to hold.

So off went the Emperor in procession under his splendid canopy. Everyone in the streets and the windows said, "Oh, how fine are the Emperor's new clothes! Don't they fit him to perfection? And see his long train!" Nobody would confess that he couldn't see anything, for that would prove him either unfit for his position, or a fool. No costume the Emperor had worn before was ever such a complete success.

"But he hasn't got anything on," a little child said. (How could a little child see the truth and have the courage to speak it out loud when no one else could? Because he saw past the beliefs of everyone else and saw the true identity - the Emperor who had no clothes on. He didn't rationalize it away and wasn't pressured by anyone to feel differently about it. So he spoke the truth.)

"Did you ever hear such innocent prattle?" said its father. (The father was caught in the belief so he tried to downplay the comment so he wouldn't be seen as anything less.) *And one person whispered to another what the child had said, "He hasn't anything on. A child says he hasn't anything on."* (If the crowd had changed the child's identity by calling it something else like "the fool, the little kid, etc" this story would have been different because they again would have fooled themselves just like they did with the swindlers/weavers.)

"But he hasn't got anything on!" the whole town cried out at last. (Truth finally came out on top - as it always eventually will.)

The Emperor shivered, for he suspected they were right. But he thought, "This procession has got to go on." So he walked more proudly than ever, as his noblemen held high the train that wasn't there at all.

So you see that the need to be seen a certain way (identity) is so powerful that it influences what we believe, think, feel, and do. It can even cause an Emperor to believe he is wearing clothes when he is really not wearing any at all.

Did you notice where his (and your) power lies in this story? It is in the conversation you have in your head. If you have prepared by daily having the right conversations reminding you who you truly are and what your values are, you will not need to debate or rationalize when you come upon a false identity or something that will go against your values. Your strong sense of self will allow you to stand up for what you know to be right. You will catch the swindlers for what they truly are and send them away before it escalates and affects the people around you.

> *"Whatever the mind can conceive and believe, it can achieve."*
>
> Napoleon Hill

If you believe it is possible, it is. You are already on your way to participating in creation - organizing things differently into something new.

The biggest hurdle is people don't truly believe something is possible. That is why they don't get the results they want.

Many people focus on what went wrong in the past (and experience depression) or focus on the unknowns of the future (and experience anxiety). Because of these focuses, people feel stuck in the present. Have you ever felt that way? Have you ever felt like you aren't going anywhere because you are too busy looking in the rearview mirror and have too much anxiety to go forward?

If people don't like their current reality they want something different and there is nothing wrong with that. The problem is that they focus on changing their behavior or the behavior of others and get frustrated when it doesn't work. They try strategy after strategy and invest in all sorts of "solutions" but it still doesn't work. They then start to doubt themselves or get frustrated. They start to think the problem must be them or the other person.

For anything to work, the focus and change must first be on yourself. You must first focus on what you can control: how you see yourself and how you see the world.

For example, you want to grow your business. But you have been trying for months now and it isn't working the way you want. You begin to fear it will never work and become depressed because it hasn't worked. You begin to doubt your ability to be a successful leader in business. You ask yourself things like, "Why can't I get this to work? When will this work? How come this is so hard? Should I try to do something else? Maybe I just wasn't cut out for this."

The key here is to have a belief that the future can be different and can be better. Even more, the key is to believe that YOU can have a different future. You have to believe you are worth it, that it can happen to you, and you can do it. If you don't believe that right now, then at least have the desire for it.

> "....A marvelous gift from the Creator: The power of the mind. The power to practically proclaim and create one's own destiny. The power to think big or to think small. The power to think positive or negative. Power to make life pay off on your own terms. Or to accept the circumstances of life and allow life to ride you.... Man has no pattern except that which he creates for himself. It can be large or small. Great or insignificant. Man controls his earthly destiny if he will use the power the Creator gave him. And do it in a spirit of belief that he can carry out his own ends."
>
> Napoleon Hill

The power of the mind

We have the opportunity to participate in the power of creation. We can create things spiritually before they are created physically. We learn this from the Bible and the original creation. God has given us a similar power and it begins in the mind. If we use this power we have the ability to create our own destiny on this Earth. We have the opportunity to decide if our lives will be extraordinary or mediocre, grand or small, if we will reach our ultimate potential, or if we will settle for the status quo.

Know that participating in the power of creation is a real power. If you think something is possible, it is. Plan it out in your mind. You activate your subconscious and it finds a way to make it possible. Then what remains is to put in the work.

Many people have created what was once "impossible":

> Thomas Edison brought about the lightbulb.
> The Wright Brothers built the first airplane.
> Elon Musk reinvented or revolutionized entire industries:
> - *PayPal - online payment system*
> - *Tesla - Electric vehicles that are now accepted and even considered luxurious!*
> - *Space X - A rocket not made by NASA!*

When you set your mind firmly on something and you believe it with complete faith, then you activate the power of the subconscious mind and allow for infinite intelligence to help you bring that to reality. If you believe in this at the depth of your core then your resolve is strengthened and your creativity is expanded. Your subconscious goes to work finding a solution.

For example, I participated in a musical production called Lamb of God. I absolutely loved it. How I felt and the testimony I gained of Jesus Christ and His life had a profound impact on how I saw myself and the world.

A year later, I was talking to one of my leaders and together we determined to put on the Lamb of God ourselves in our area. I felt so strongly about the production that I thought, "Sure, we can make it happen! I just have to copy the formula that worked before and make it happen." I didn't even think about how hard it might be, or the fact that I had never done something like this before, or what everyone else would think, etc.

I had a *certainty* that this would work. I had a passion for making it work because I believed in the power of what it could do for the people who would participate.

I took on this challenge while I was working full-time. I faced the frustrations. Even when it didn't seem like we were getting enough people for the choir and it could appear discouraging and I could allow for thoughts to come in saying, "Is this going to work? Maybe you should change your mind. Maybe you should stop and do something else that is easier?" I quickly overcame thoughts like that because of my firm faith, my strong belief, my feeling of certainty, and how I had set my mind on making this happen. I had already chosen a date. We had already booked the venue.

I continued to press forward. I used the power of prayer. I prayed with more fervor than I did at other times in my life because I knew this had to happen and I knew that I did not know how to do it on my own. I knew that I needed His help. I knew that this was His work and so I knew that I needed His extra power.

As I did this I was inspired to reach out to others. As I reached out to others they gave me ideas and I continued to know that I could not and should not do this on my own - that others were willing to help. There were others already in place to help make this happen and to help accomplish amazing things. In two months we produced a 90-minute show with narrators and soloists, a choir, a full orchestra, and directors. We performed three shows and had nearly 3,000 people attend.

It is amazing what we can accomplish when our mind is set.

Focus, Meaning, Emotion

How are you setting yourself up for success with the things you focus on?

It is easy to get caught up in what isn't working, what could go wrong, and what you don't want to happen. But you must remember to focus on what you DO want.

In sports, you frequently hear coaches telling players to "Keep your eye on the ball!" If you are playing football and put your energy towards avoiding getting tackled by the other team, rather than focusing on catching the ball, then chances are you won't catch it. On the other hand, if you focus on catching the ball, you will likely catch it, then you will be better prepared to absorb the tackle or dodge it completely.

If you focus your energy on what you want, you will drive towards it with energy and purpose. If you focus on what you don't want, you will fall back trying to avoid those things.

How do you want to show up when facing your challenges?

Another example is when mountain biking down a mountain, you can get upwards of 30 mph. If you hit a large enough rock when going that fast, you could stumble and get really hurt. The natural thing would be to look out for all the rocks and try to avoid them. But if you stare at all the rocks, you will steer towards them. The key is to focus not on where you don't want to go, but where you do want to go. Focus on the safe areas of the path. You will go there because that is where your focus is.

You make three decisions all day every day:

    1. What you focus on

    2. What meaning you assign

    3. What emotion you feel

Take the example of a glass with water in it. If you focus on the empty half, you decide the glass is half empty and that your child must have spilled some of it again (meaning), and your emotion is one of frustration.

If you focus on the full half, you decide that the glass is half full since your child hasn't spilled the drink today, and your emotion is gratitude.

The cup and situation are the same, yet your experience can be completely different based of your focus and meaning.

Try this for yourself. Practice noticing these three decisions that you make all day every day. It can help to start backwards if necessary. You can pause and ask yourself, "What am I feeling right now?" Or you can think of a situation in the past and recall what you felt then. Then ask yourself "Why am I feeling that emotion? What meaning am I assigning that makes me feel this way? What am I focusing on that is causing this?"

Let's say you realize that you are discouraged and unmotivated (emotion). Why? Because you went to some networking events and talked to a lot of people but you haven't gotten any new business. You think it was a waste of time to go to those events because they obviously didn't work (meaning). Where is your focus? On the lack of results.

If you change your focus to the fact that you met three new people and can call them later to continue your conversation from earlier, then change your meaning to be that you can build relationships with these people that may eventually lead into business but at a minimum you made three new friends, then you will feel happy, grateful, and accomplished from going to those networking events.

Where your focus goes, energy flows. When you focus on what isn't working or hasn't worked, you will be stressed or depressed. If you focus on what lies in your power, you feel empowered to change something about your life. That brings fulfillment and happiness.

Do you focus on the 88 people who said no or the 12 people who said yes?

If you are 99% certain this will work, do you focus on that or do you focus on the 1% chance it might not?

Do you focus on all that still needs to get done or do you acknowledge and celebrate the things you did get done today?

Another way of saying Focus, Meaning, and Emotion is, "What you see, how you interpret it, and how you react."

There was a woman who would often go climbing with her husband. One day, she fell while climbing and lost nearly 100% of the use of her legs. Although she did have to make some changes in her life like moving into a house that is more accessible for her, she didn't let this event ruin her life. She decided she would still enjoy the outdoors and that she wanted to hike. She had an adaptive 3-wheeled bike made where she could sit and lean forward and use her hands to pedal and brake.

My family went on a hike with her and her family. It was amazing to watch her on the bike - especially as she went up and down some very steep switchbacks. Some switchbacks were too narrow for her to make it on her bike so we had to lift the bike and turn her so she could fit. At times it was slow going and other people on the trail had to wait for us. I never heard a single complaint or even a look of frustration from the people who had to wait on the trail. On the contrary, I heard many comments like, "So inspiring!" "You got this!" "Incredible!"

As I watched this happen, I was impressed by how our focus determines our attitude. The switchbacks were steep and it was pretty hot. Most people could have been sweaty, tired, and frustrated if something were to slow them down. But when everyone's focus was on how someone with limited ability had found a way to get up the mountain, they forgot about all their own discomforts and felt inspired instead.

We see or experience what we expect to see

Let's say you just bought a brand new, bright red Corvette. You had been saving up for it for quite some time and you were finally able to purchase your dream car. You were sure that nobody else had this car so you were excited to take your unique car home.

As you drive it home, you see another one on the freeway. You see one at the grocery store. It turns out that someone who lives on your block also has one! How did you not notice it before?

This is the classic example of never noticing something until you focus on it.

On the contrary, you didn't notice all the Subaru's on the road. Why? Because they weren't part of your focus.

The same thing applies to worry. If you focus on worry, you will find it. If you focus on what you can control, even though some things that might cause worry still exist, you will feel much better.

Is it really this simple?

Do you mean to say that I can choose to control how I feel and thus dispel depression, anxiety, and even things like high blood pressure and stomach ulcers?

Yes. Dale Carnegie and many others had figured it out in the early 1900's. In his book, "Stop Worrying and Start Living" Carnegie teaches 10 ways to conquer worry. A lot of them have to do with what you choose to focus on.

If you focus on the future and what you cannot control you are bound to feel stress.

If you focus on things that worry you, you are bound to feel worried.

In today's world, we just look for a pill to swallow and expect our problems to magically disappear. But what happens when the pill wears off? Has the problem been solved? If not, is the pill the solution?

"No, but it makes me feel better!"

"Feeling" better leads to addiction.

"Being" better leads to recovery and healing.

Being better requires you to make an internal change while "feeling" better requires you to use something external.

Our brains are hardwired to look for threats. That is why we can find and focus so easily on what is wrong with life. But doing so also brings feelings of uncertainty and lack of confidence. Learn to redirect your focus to see past the threats and enjoy life.

What you focus on expands. What are you allowing yourself to focus on?

Whatever we choose to focus on is what we end up seeing.

Practicing Gratitude

Gratitude is the practice of being thankful for what you have, rather than focusing on what you don't have. Gratitude has been shown to improve overall well-being and happiness. In this section, we will explore habits that can help you practice gratitude, including keeping a gratitude journal, expressing gratitude to others, and focusing on the present moment.

Practicing Gratitude for a Happier Life

Gratitude is a powerful tool for promoting happiness and well-being and has been shown to have numerous benefits for mental and physical health.

Why Practice Gratitude?

Research has shown that regularly practicing gratitude can help to:

- Increase happiness and positive emotions
- Reduce stress and anxiety
- Improve sleep quality
- Strengthen relationships
- Boost immune system function
- Increase resilience in the face of challenges

The Science of Gratitude

Gratitude works by changing our perspective and focus. When we intentionally focus on the good things in life and express gratitude for them, we train our minds to see the positive aspects of our experiences. This helps to shift our attention away from negative thoughts and emotions and towards positive ones.

Practicing gratitude also has a neurochemical effect on the brain. It has been shown to increase levels of dopamine and serotonin, neurotransmitters that play a key role in regulating mood and emotions. This can lead to increased feelings of happiness and well-being.

Practical Ways to Practice Gratitude

There are many ways to practice gratitude, and it doesn't have to be complicated or time-consuming. Here are some simple but effective ways to incorporate gratitude into your daily routine:

Keep a Gratitude Journal: Take a few minutes each day to write down three things you are grateful for. This could be anything from a sunny day to a kind gesture from a friend. Reflecting on the good things in your life can help you cultivate a more positive outlook.

At the end of each day, you get to decide what kind of day you had. You can reframe what happened and choose your perspective. Did it suck or did you grow? Did you learn?

One day a man received a $3,000 bonus at work. He was elated! He thought, "This is great! God must love me." When he got home he found out that his furnace stopped working and he had to replace it. Guess how much it cost? $3,000! He was disappointed, frustrated, and discouraged. "This sucks. I can't believe this happened - especially when I was having a good day. God must hate me."

At the end of the day, this man had a habit of keeping a gratitude journal. Keeping that journal always helped him check his perspective. As he wrote, he realized that the very same day his furnace went out, he received a bonus at work for that exact amount. How incredibly blessed he was! He was filled with deep gratitude. "God must really love me because he knew this would happen and made sure I had a way to handle it."

Do you see the power of gratitude here? The man experienced strong emotions of joy as well as disappointment that day. He could have let that disappointment carry with him for a while and let it taint his relationship with God and give him a different view towards bonuses. He could have even associated disaster with a bonus! If he had that association, any future bonus would make him think he is going to find an expensive disaster at home. But because he took time to feel gratitude, he was able to reframe this experience into something empowering. The meaning he found and was grateful for was that he is being watched over and is very blessed.

Express Gratitude to Others

Take time to thank the people in your life who have made a difference. Write a thank-you note, send a text, or simply say thank you in person. Expressing gratitude to others can strengthen relationships and increase feelings of connection and happiness.

Practice Mindfulness

Take a few minutes each day to focus on the present moment and notice the good things around you. This could be as simple as savoring your morning meal or enjoying a beautiful sunset. Mindfulness can help you cultivate a greater sense of appreciation for the present moment.

Find Joy in the Small Things

Take time to appreciate the small moments of joy in your life. This could be anything from a good book to a favorite song. Paying attention to the small pleasures in life can help you cultivate a sense of gratitude for the everyday.

Cultivate a Gratitude Mindset: Shift your focus from what you don't have to what you do have. Rather than focusing on what is lacking, focus on the abundance in your life. This can help you cultivate a mindset of gratitude and appreciation.

I had a client apply these steps of gratitude and it made a big change in her life. She had a tendency to be very negative and had pretty crappy days as a result. While working with me, she decided to start a gratitude journal and she wrote in it at the end of each day. Doing this allowed her to completely shift her perspective of the entire day. While she used to end the day saying it sucked, she found things she was grateful for and realized it was a much better day than she realized. She began to discover how many good things happened each day. As she focused on those and felt gratitude for them, she naturally started to see the positive things more often. She saw more things as possible. Her demeanor and attitude changed. She even started helping her husband see and be more positive. She saw herself and her world differently.

Gratitude is to set your mind on positive things - things you are grateful for. What does that do for you? It gives you a perspective of yourself in comparison to the world. You no longer see yourself in the light of "I don't have enough, I don't have what my neighbor has, I will never have enough" and all those debilitating and unhelpful thoughts. Rather, you realize all of the things that you do have.

During Covid-19, when the world was shutting down, people were afraid, contention was building, and uncertainty abounded. President Russel M Nelson, a world-renowned heart surgeon as well as a prophet of God, gave a message to the world. He described how as a man of science he realized all of the work that was going into developing a vaccine for the virus. Efforts were being made to help people on a physical level. The physical virus was not the only issue in the world. He knew there was hatred and fear and anxiety and contention. Of all the advice he could give, as a doctor, prophet, and father, the prescription that he gave was the power of gratitude - to think of what you are grateful for and to share with others.

I invite you to do the same right now. Share either on social media or out loud with a loved one something that you are grateful for each day. Keep a journal and note how you feel at the end of each day after you share your gratitude. If you do this you will notice a change in your emotional state.

You can only feel one emotion at a time. If you feel grateful you cannot feel scared, worried, or uncertain. Feeling grateful will lead to you feeling more confidence, more peace, and more calm.

Practicing gratitude is a simple but powerful practice that can have a profound impact on our well-being. By taking time to reflect on the good things in our lives, we can cultivate a more positive outlook and increase our feelings of happiness and connection. Incorporate these practical gratitude practices into your daily routine, and see how they can positively impact your life.

Focusing on what you want and applying what you just read will strengthen your belief.

Believe in yourself

Your success in life comes from belief in yourself. It starts with focusing on the right things and focusing your energy to make them happen. You must visualize your desired future and see yourself there.

Belief is powerful; belief in yourself, belief in a higher power. Belief defines the thoughts you have and keep.

The way we talk to ourselves influences what we believe about ourselves

Here is an example of the power that small modifications to your language (both inward and outward) can have.

You may consider the future in thoughts like this: "I hope that one day I have a successful business. That sure would be nice."

What kind of emotions do you feel when you read these things? Apprehension? Stress? Anxiety?

Now change the thoughts to: "I have a successful business. I am so happy!"

What kind of emotions do you feel when you read these? Do you feel excited? Do you feel like it is possible? Do you feel powerful?

The change that was made is (1) putting them in I AM statements and (2) putting them in present tense.

Talking to yourself in this way causes your self-concept to change.

At first, you may not fully believe that it's possible, but you have this nervous excitement and you proceed not knowing how it will happen.

The power of the brain is amazing. If you can activate your subconscious and have your brain work for you even when you're not consciously putting forth the effort, you can accomplish amazing things.

Your brain cannot tell the difference between something vividly imagined and reality. If you can activate this power and use it to your advantage you can vividly imagine a desired future and your brain will already believe that it is reality. It will activate its reticular activating system and will begin to look for all the ways and all opportunities to make this come to pass.

Let me tell you from personal experience, multiple times, and from helping many clients, that when done correctly this works! The key here is that because you are talking to yourself and about yourself differently and in empowering ways, your sense of self changes. You start to believe in yourself. You start to believe that you are capable and because you have this sense of belief, your thoughts change, your emotions stay positive, and you behave in ways that you know you should which will lead to the results that you want. This all happens on a subconscious level because you have done it the right way. Then this cycle is positive and becomes self-reinforcing.

The Power of Visualization

Visualization is a powerful technique that involves using your imagination to create mental images of positive outcomes or goals you want to achieve. By visualizing a desired outcome in vivid detail, you can create a powerful belief and sense of motivation, focus, and confidence that can help you take action and achieve your goals.

Here are some ways in which visualization can be a powerful tool for personal growth and achievement:

1. Enhancing Motivation: By visualizing yourself achieving a goal, you create a mental image of success that can inspire you to take action and persist in the face of obstacles.

2. Boosting Confidence: By imagining yourself accomplishing a difficult task or overcoming an obstacle, you can create a sense of self-efficacy and belief in your own abilities.

3. Reducing Anxiety: By imagining yourself in a calm and peaceful state, you can create a sense of relaxation and reduce feelings of stress and tension.

4. Improving Performance: Visualization has been used by athletes and performers to improve their performance. By visualizing themselves performing at a high level, they can create a mental blueprint for success that can help them achieve their goals.

5. Enhancing Creativity: By visualizing new and innovative ideas, you can create a mental image of a desired outcome that can inspire you to think outside the box and come up with creative solutions to problems.

The key to visualization is to put yourself where you want to be. Imagine yourself actually there, already having accomplished it. Become that person. If you don't know all the "how" of accomplishing it, just focus on the result you want. Put yourself there emotionally. If you can vividly imagine it, your brain knows it is possible because it thinks it has already experienced it. So it activates the power of the subconscious and finds ways to make that imagined reality an actual reality.

Visualize yourself achieving your result and becoming that person. Repeat this visualization exercise regularly, and make it a part of your daily routine. Over time, you will find that visualization can become a powerful tool for personal growth and achievement, helping you to create the future you desire.

The ability to foresee obstacles is powerful. When you do this, they no longer have the power to discourage or distract you because you have seen them from afar and you are ready for them. What used to knock you off your feet is now an obstacle that you face head on. You already have a plan for how you will go around it, over it, under it, through it, or embrace it. You will have planned for success rather than hoped to not fail.

Summary of Chapter 6

- Belief in oneself and the possibility of change is a fundamental key to achieving success and personal growth. It involves focusing on what you want, rather than what you don't want, and cultivating a mindset of gratitude.

- Focusing on the positive aspects of life and expressing gratitude can lead to increased happiness, reduced stress, improved relationships, and overall well-being.

- Visualization is a powerful technique that involves imagining yourself already achieving your goals. This practice enhances motivation, boosts confidence, reduces anxiety, improves performance, and enhances creativity.

Questions for Application:

- How can you incorporate a daily gratitude practice into your routine to shift your focus towards positive aspects of your life?

- Think of a specific goal you want to achieve. How can you apply visualization to vividly imagine yourself already having accomplished that goal? How does this visualization affect your belief in its achievability?

- Reflect on a recent situation where you faced an obstacle. How would your approach to overcoming it change if you had visualized and prepared for it in advance? How can you use this foresight to approach future challenges with confidence and determination?

Chapter 7 - Thoughts: What Do You Think About Yourself?

The Access Point

Mindset

The conversations you have in your head

Stories you tell yourself

Self Talk

Thoughts are where the subconscious meets the conscious

"Be careful how you talk to yourself. You are likely to believe it."

> *One thing you have full control over is the power of thought. Nobody controls this but you.*

The key to reaching your ultimate potential lies in mastering the power of thought. Acknowledge how powerful your thoughts are, and you will unlock potential you may not have known was there.

You want more for your life. You feel it. You are called to it. You know there is more. That is your potential. You strive to reach it - to make it real. You have these moments of clarity and inspiration. Other times you are overwhelmed by negative thoughts.

A powerful way to master the power of thought is to harness the power of positive self-talk.

This section is designed to provide you with a comprehensive guide to the power of positive self-talk. It offers practical techniques and strategies for developing a more positive mindset, building confidence, improving relationships, and overcoming obstacles. By incorporating positive self-talk into your daily life, you can achieve your goals, overcome your limiting beliefs, and reach your ultimate potential.

Introduction to Positive Self-Talk: How to Transform Your Inner Dialogue

The way we talk to ourselves has a significant impact on our mental and emotional well-being. Negative self-talk can cause feelings of anxiety, low self-esteem, and self-doubt, while positive self-talk can increase our confidence, motivation, and overall sense of happiness. In this section, we will explore the concept of positive self-talk, its benefits, and how to use it to transform your inner dialogue.

Notice how you are talking to yourself as you read this. Are you saying things like, "This is great! So true! Wow!" or are you saying things like, "No way, this doesn't make sense, how can this be true?" See? You already noticed the fact you talk to yourself all the time!

What is Positive Self-Talk?

Positive self-talk is a technique that involves using positive, affirming language to speak to yourself. It is about recognizing and acknowledging your strengths, abilities, and accomplishments, rather than focusing on your weaknesses and failures. Positive self-talk can help you develop a more optimistic outlook on life, build self-confidence, and enhance your overall well-being.

Self-talk doesn't have to be about yourself. It is how you talk to yourself in general.

The Benefits of Positive Self-Talk

There are several benefits to using positive self-talk, including:

1. Increased Self-Confidence: Positive self-talk can help you believe in yourself and your abilities.

2. Reduced Stress and Anxiety: By using positive language to speak to yourself, you can reduce feelings of stress and anxiety.

3. Improved Focus: Positive self-talk can help you maintain focus and stay motivated, even during challenging times.

4. Better Relationships: Positive self-talk can improve your relationships with others by helping you communicate more effectively and positively.

How to Use Positive Self-Talk

Here are some tips for using positive self-talk:

1. Be Mindful: Pay attention to your thoughts and notice when you are engaging in negative self-talk. Reframe negative thoughts into positive ones.

2. Use Affirmations: Use affirmations to affirm positive beliefs about yourself. Examples include "I am capable," "I am strong," and "I am worthy."

3. Practice Gratitude: Focus on the positive things in your life and express gratitude for them. This can help shift your mindset towards positivity.

4. Be Kind to Yourself: Treat yourself with kindness and compassion, just as you would a friend or loved one. Remember that nobody is perfect, and it's okay to make mistakes.

Positive self-talk is a powerful tool for transforming your inner dialogue and improving your overall well-being. By using positive, affirming language to speak to yourself, you can increase your self-confidence, reduce feelings of stress and anxiety, and maintain focus and motivation. Remember to be mindful of your thoughts, use affirmations, practice gratitude, and be kind to yourself. With practice, positive self-talk can become a natural part of your inner dialogue, helping you live a more positive and fulfilling life.

I have a client who is both a mortgage broker and a real estate agent. This year has been difficult for him; he's had to work harder than ever before in the 26 years since he was first licensed. Customers have not come to him as easily as they used to.

He came to me for help with his self-talk. He would constantly talk to himself negatively. He would see all the negatives in his life and blame himself for them. He struggled to see much good in his life, let alone about himself.

Through our sessions, he learned a technique that has helped him implement positive self-talk into his life. He learned to reframe negative things into positive things.

He wanted to make sure he did it every day and this worked so well that he even gave himself a "prescription" as if he were his own Positive Self-Talk doctor and put it on his monitor.

> Prescription: "Reframe to Positive."

> Clap hands as the physical trigger to flip from negative to positive.

> Connect to the love of connecting with others.

When he had a day with no calls on his schedule, rather than getting discouraged and talking negatively to himself, he would do the following:

> Notice the negative thought.

Clap his hands once and flip the thought into something positive.

Connect it with something he loves.

So when he had no calls, he did the exercise like this:

"No calls?" (Clap) "Great! Now I have time to make calls. This helps me connect with people. And I love connecting with people!"

Because he does this, he quickly gets out of his old negative thinking. This new perspective and momentum have helped him get new business, solve problems in his business, and give him optimism for how his business will do this year.

The Power of Words: How to Use Language to Empower Yourself and Others

"Are words a little bit powerful or a lot a bit powerful?"
                                                    Brad Barton

Words are an essential aspect of our lives and have the power to shape our thoughts, beliefs, and emotions. They can inspire us to greatness or drag us down into despair. They play a significant role in shaping our perception of ourselves and others. Whether they uplift us or bring us down, words play a vital role in our daily interactions.

This section will explore the impact of words on our lives and how we can use them as tools to empower ourselves and others.

The Impact of Words

Negative words can demotivate us, instill fear, and limit our potential. They can cause us to doubt ourselves and our abilities, leading to low self-esteem and a lack of confidence.

Why do words hurt? Because they influence our thoughts and we use our thoughts to talk to ourselves.

If you first gain the power to check your words, you will then begin to have the power to check your judgment, and at length actually gain the power to check your thoughts and reflections.

How do you change your thoughts? Listen to the internal script in your mind. If you don't like your current thoughts, erase them and replace them with other thoughts. It takes practice, but it is possible. The process is even more effective when you have someone help you.

Positive words, on the other hand, can uplift and inspire us, encouraging us to pursue our dreams and reach our full potential.

As soon as you think something is possible, it becomes such. When you begin to talk about it, you are participating in the beginning of creation. There is literal power and energy in your words.

Using Language to Empower Yourself

Language can be a powerful tool for self-empowerment. By using positive and empowering language, we can boost our self-esteem, increase our confidence, and achieve our goals. Here are some ways to use language to empower yourself:

1. Positive Self-Talk: Speak to yourself positively and use words of encouragement and affirmation. This can help you believe in yourself and your abilities.

> One of my boys experienced positive self-talk while playing flag football. At first, he really hated flag football and was pretty down on himself because he had been struggling to catch the ball in the rare moments that it was passed to him. We talked one night about the power of positive self-talk and he decided to try it. Instead of constantly telling himself he was bad at football and would never catch the ball, he learned to imagine himself catching the ball and how good he would feel when that happened. Then he summarized that feeling with some positive self-talk. "I can do this! I got this!" The very next game, he caught the ball and scored a touchdown!

Change the way you talk to yourself and the things you experience will change. You will get different results.

2. Reframing: Reframe negative thoughts into positive ones. Instead of saying "I can't do it," say "I will try my best."

3. Affirmations: Use affirmations to affirm positive beliefs about yourself. Examples include "I am capable," "I am strong," and "I am worthy."

4. Visualization: Visualize success and positive outcomes. This can help you create a positive mindset and improve your self-confidence.

Using Language to Empower Others

Language can also be a powerful tool for empowering others. By using positive and empowering language with others, we can motivate and encourage them to reach their ultimate potential. Here are some ways to use language to empower others:

1. Encouragement: Encourage others by providing positive feedback and words of encouragement. This can help boost their self-esteem and confidence.

2. Validation: Validate others by acknowledging their feelings and experiences. This can help them feel heard and understood.

3. Empathy: Show empathy by putting yourself in someone else's shoes. This can help build trust and strengthen relationships.

4. Inspirational Speech: Use language to inspire and motivate others. Deliver a motivational speech or share inspiring stories to uplift and encourage them.

Bonus: Try using this empowering language with the person you see in the mirror.

The power of words cannot be underestimated. The words we use can have a profound impact on our lives and the lives of those around us. By using positive and empowering language, we can boost our self-esteem, increase our confidence, and motivate ourselves and others to reach our full potential. Remember, words have the power to uplift and inspire, use them wisely.

Identifying Negative Self-Talk: How to Recognize and Overcome Self-Defeating Thoughts

Negative self-talk is a common problem that can hinder personal growth and well-being. It can lead to feelings of low self-esteem, anxiety, and self-doubt. In this section, we will explore the concept of negative self-talk, its impact on our lives, and how to recognize and overcome it.

What is Negative Self-Talk?

Negative self-talk refers to the critical or self-defeating thoughts that we have about ourselves. These thoughts can be conscious or unconscious, and they can affect our emotions, behaviors, and overall sense of well-being. Negative self-talk often involves distorted or exaggerated thinking patterns, such as catastrophizing or black-and-white thinking.

The Impact of Negative Self-Talk

Negative self-talk can have a profound impact on our lives, including:

1. Low Self-Esteem: Negative self-talk can lead to feelings of low self-esteem, making it difficult to believe in ourselves and our abilities.

2. Anxiety and Depression: Negative self-talk can contribute to feelings of anxiety and depression, leading to a sense of hopelessness and helplessness.

3. Poor Decision-Making: Negative self-talk can cloud our judgment, leading to poor decision-making and ineffective problem-solving.

4. Limited Beliefs: Negative self-talk can create limiting beliefs that hold us back from achieving our goals and living up to our full potential.

Self-critical thoughts make you critical of others. If you can't be perfect inside you expect everything outside you to be perfect.

Sometimes you might slip up and allow unhelpful thoughts to spend free time in your head. Maybe you won't keep commitments to yourself. Maybe your choices won't honor your true identity. When these things happen, you begin to have intense conversations inside your head. You know what you did. Do you admit it? Do you face it? Or do you rationalize it away?

Examine your thoughts. Can you look at this another way? What would a reasonable person think of this?

How to Recognize Negative Self-Talk

1. You use harsh, critical language when speaking to yourself.

2. You focus on your weaknesses and failures, rather than your strengths and accomplishments.

3. You have a tendency to catastrophize or jump to worst-case scenarios.

4. You engage in black-and-white thinking, seeing things as all-good or all-bad, with no gray area in between.

5. You feel discouraged, unmotivated, like nothing will work, etc.

Overcoming Negative Self-Talk

1. Identify Triggers: Pay attention to the situations or events that trigger negative self-talk, and try to avoid or minimize them.

2. Practice Mindfulness: Practice being mindful of your thoughts and feelings, and challenge negative thoughts as they arise.

3. Use Positive Affirmations: Use positive affirmations to replace negative self-talk with positive, affirming language.

4. Seek Support: Reach out to friends, family, or a mental health professional for support and guidance. This is where good therapy and/or good coaching come into play. They are trained to know how to help reprogram your brain.

5. Say the opposite. When one of my clients first started working with me she described herself as "naturally pessimistic and anxious." We talked about how talking about herself in that manner was affecting her in disempowering ways. I helped her reframe those words and she changed it to "I have a tendency to be pessimistic and I experience anxiety at times."

Can you feel a difference in those words? Just saying it that way took the idea from a description of who she was to simply a behavior she experiences. This difference was so powerful for her that she began coming to sessions with a smile that showed her inner confidence. She helped her husband reframe how he talked about himself and it has been a great change for their relationship.

What kinds of conversations would she have with herself if she kept the identity of "naturally pessimistic and anxious?"

How would it be different if she moved this identifying belief into a simple behavior of having a "tendency to be pessimistic and experience anxiety at times?"

Negative self-talk is a common problem that can have a profound impact on our lives. By recognizing the signs of negative self-talk and learning strategies to overcome it, we can improve our self-esteem, reduce feelings of anxiety and depression, and live up to our full potential. Remember to be mindful of your thoughts, use positive affirmations, and seek support when needed. With practice, you can transform your inner dialogue and achieve a more positive and fulfilling life.

The Voices in Your Head

Why do we like to dilute our power of the mind and distract ourselves so much with mind-numbing things like dumb YouTube videos? You know, the cat videos?

One reason is that if we haven't learned to control the voices in our head, then most of our thoughts are heavy and painful. We don't like to feel that way so we turn to anything else. We are slowly chipping away at our self-concept.

You have the power to choose your thoughts. But where do all the different thoughts come from? Are they generated within yourself, or externally? If you choose your thoughts, why do random ones appear in your mind? Where do the unrelated, inappropriate, distracting, and deceptive thoughts originate from? How do you know which ones are beneficial and which are harmful?

Did you know there are three voices in your head? (Some of you may be thinking. "Only three? I have a lot more than that!")

Consider this: You have three voices in your head and these three voices give opinions on the thoughts inside your head. You make the ultimate decision on which voice you will follow.

The main thing you hear in your head is your own inner voice. Generally, this voice will be encouraging because you want to make yourself feel good, achieve the goals you set for yourself, and get the most out of life. You tell yourself that life is good and you are doing a great job. When you have an idea or plan, this inner voice will motivate and push you to start working on it with determination. This is how you begin the journey.

Then there are two other voices entering your mind.

One is positive, coming from a good source: some people call it the universe, I call it God. God understands your full potential and knows what you can do, as well as the things you will have to overcome. His reassuring thoughts offer guidance to help you get to a place of ultimate joy and satisfaction. If you pay attention to these encouraging thoughts, achieving success will come faster and easier. Feelings of peace, joy, and calm accompany these ideas.

The third voice, the one that tells you all the negative things, springs from a negative source. He is sometimes referred to as your "inner critic" but he is actually the devil himself. He knows exactly what you are capable of and will do whatever he can to keep you from achieving your goals. He attempts to distract, discourage, and deceive you. He convinces you of all the reasons why it isn't wise for you to go after something, reminding you of past failures. He whispers that you are not worthy enough to reach for your dreams and that you don't deserve whatever it is you are striving for. He fills your mind with distractions and all of the other things that could occupy your time instead. He uses your emotional pain and insecurities to make you feel alone and make you withdraw from people.

Voice	Message	Thoughts	Signs
Yours (inner voice)	Generally positive	I got this. I am pretty sure I know enough. I am trying my best.	Generally confident.
God's	Always empowering	You are amazing. You have more potential than you realize. I am here for you. You will succeed.	Peace. Resolve. Assurance. Clarity.
Satan's (inner critic)	Always deceptive, discouraging, and destructive	You are not good enough. This will never work. Why even try? You are a failure.	Confusion. Fear. Discouragement.

I used to think that the negative thoughts came from my own head, but that goes to show you how sneaky the devil is. He speaks to you in a voice that sounds exactly like your own. That is why you don't recognize him for who he is! He comes in so smoothly and so quickly that you think it is your own voice making the arguments. They make so much sense that we struggle not to believe them.

What you observe and hear, experiences from your past, books you read, how you talk to yourself - all of these sources matter. Negative thinking can stem from outside influences like news outlets, social media platforms, failures or setbacks, etc. Get used to pushing them away. Realize that they're not good for you. Analyze the thought and where it comes from before accepting it as true. If the source is corrupted, the words will be corrupted - so cast them out of your mind! You can't drink dirty water and expect not to get sick. Decide what you allow into your mind. Pay attention to who is speaking into your life. Manage your influencers.

Your mind is like a stage. Many thoughts will be vying for that space and attention, but there is only room for one thought on that stage at a time. God wants to help you with those decisions. Satan does as well. The good news is, <u>you are the stage director.</u> You get to decide which voice you listen to and which thought remains on that stage.

The key is to realize that you can observe your thoughts without believing them at face value. You can discern them with the knowledge that sometimes a thought that makes a ton of sense and yet is a hurtful idea actually comes from Satan (not you - even though it sounds like it came from you). When you realize this, you can team up with God and cast out Satan, giving you the power to make better decisions.

One way to help you discern these voices is to uncover the accurate facts in observing thoughts. Ask, "How do you know this is true? What evidence do you have?" Note the bias of the person talking.

For example, as I was writing this book I had this resolve to write every morning from 6:30 to 7:30. If I simply stuck with my commitment (my voice) I would just wake up and write at 6:30. Nothing would stop me. I was aligned with God's voice which helped me know that this book would be a good thing for many people. But what would have happened if I paused to consider and possibly rationalize the possibility of not writing at 6:30 in the morning? I would have come up with all sorts of ideas (devil's voice) - namely the fact that we hadn't gone to bed super early the previous night, the fact that I had allergies and it made me more tired, the fact that it was warm the last night and maybe I hadn't slept super well, that the kids were awake, etc. All of these ideas were valid. In fact, they were all true! Therefore they could have felt pretty good. I could have felt like I was justified in not keeping my commitment to myself. I could have just slept in. This small idea, just a small thing, could have delayed my writing and made sure that it did not happen as I had committed myself to do.

Now you may ask yourself, "What's wrong with all these thoughts? How do you know that these thoughts are coming from the devil?"

I fully realize that these thoughts sound like my own. When it seems like you are coming up with all these negative thoughts, they are actually negative thoughts coming from the devil. His goal is to make you miserable. That is his one and only motive.

This is where you have to pause and not just believe all the thoughts at face value. You have to step back and ask yourself questions.

Do this exercise with me. Ask yourself, "What result will I get if I believe these thoughts? Will I accomplish my goal? Is this helping me keep my commitment? How do I feel about these thoughts? How will I feel about my behavior 24 hours from now?"

So when you ask yourself these questions and you think "Where are these thoughts taking me?" then you can know that they are not taking you to your commitment. And as you observe those thoughts you think, "These certainly wouldn't come from me because I know that I have made a commitment with myself, and I am willing to do whatever is necessary to make this happen. Therefore these thoughts that are telling me not to keep my commitment to myself must be coming from the devil. With that being the case I will cast the devil out and get to work. I will invoke the power of God and positive thoughts to make my actions a reality and to empower my efforts so that what Satan tries to stop me from doing will be an even bigger force for good. After all, why would Satan be trying to stop me if I wasn't doing something worthwhile?"

See how the right questions help you have the right conversations with yourself? The right conversation in your mind will help you feel empowering emotions that encourage you to act in a way that will get you the result you want. If you aren't getting the results you want, it is because the wrong conversations are happening inside your head. Change the story you tell yourself and you will change everything else.

There are so many voices out there. Which one do you listen to most often? Do you know what the voice of God sounds like? Can you recognize it when it is speaking?

Did you know there were these three different voices in your head? How does this knowledge affect you?

Developing a Positive Mindset: How to Cultivate a Growth Mindset and Harness the Power of Positivity

A positive mindset can have a profound impact on our lives, allowing us to approach challenges with optimism, resilience, and creativity. In this section, we will explore the concept of a positive mindset, its benefits, and how to cultivate it.

What is a Positive Mindset?

A positive mindset is a way of thinking that focuses on opportunities rather than obstacles and emphasizes the good in a situation rather than the bad. It is a way of looking at the world with optimism and approaching challenges with a can-do attitude.

A positive mindset is characterized by positive self-talk, a growth mindset, and an emphasis on gratitude and positivity. This is not toxic positivity. It is not fooling yourself to believe life is perfect or there is nothing negative in life. But it is choosing to direct your focus to the positives that exist all around you. It is choosing to direct your focus to what is helpful rather than unhelpful.

The Benefits of a Positive Mindset

A positive mindset has many benefits, including:

1. Improved Resilience: A positive mindset helps us bounce back from setbacks and challenges, allowing us to recover quickly and move forward with optimism.

2. Increased Creativity: A positive mindset encourages us to think outside the box and approach problems with a sense of curiosity and exploration, leading to increased creativity and innovation.

3. Improved Relationships: A positive mindset helps us to build stronger, more positive relationships with others, as we approach them with empathy, kindness, and understanding.

4. Better Health: A positive mindset has been linked to better physical and mental health outcomes, including reduced stress, improved immune function, and reduced risk of depression and anxiety.

How to Cultivate a Positive Mindset

Here are some strategies for cultivating a positive mindset:

1. Practice Positive Self-Talk: Pay attention to the language you use when speaking to yourself, and replace negative self-talk with positive, affirming language.

2. Embrace Failure and Growth: Adopt a growth mindset, and approach challenges as opportunities for learning and growth.

3. Focus on Gratitude: Practice gratitude by reflecting on the positive aspects of your life and expressing appreciation for the people and things that bring you joy.

4. Surround Yourself with Positivity: Surround yourself with positive people, media, and experiences that inspire and uplift you.

5. Celebrate Your Wins - Keep a journal of good things that happen each day.

Another way to program your positive mindset is to do things that are more easily visible. Do things you can see and enjoy. If you enjoy playing the piano and it makes you feel accomplished, play it more often! Program things into your life that make you feel good, and speak positively about yourself. Doing so will help increase your ability to habitually have a positive mindset.

Having a positive mindset gives you a filter that "everything is possible." When you get into this emotional state of mind, you easily come up with great ideas - as opposed to being stuck.

Here are some examples of people who have exhibited positive mindsets and what they were able to do:

1. Nick Vujicic - Nick was born without arms or legs, but he doesn't let his physical limitations hold him back. He's become a motivational speaker, sharing his story and message of hope with people around the world. He focuses on the things he can do, rather than what he can't, and encourages others to do the same.

2. J.K. Rowling - J.K. Rowling was a struggling single mother living on welfare when she wrote the first Harry Potter book. Despite facing rejection from numerous (12) publishers, Rowling refused to give up on her dream. She continued to believe in herself and her story, eventually finding a publisher who saw the potential in her work. Today, Rowling is one of the most successful authors of all time, inspiring millions of readers with her stories of hope, courage, and magic.

3. Richard Branson - Richard Branson is the founder of the Virgin Group, a conglomerate of companies that includes Virgin Records, Virgin Airlines, and Virgin Galactic. He's known for his positive outlook and willingness to take risks. Even when faced with setbacks or failures, he maintains a can-do attitude and looks for new opportunities.

4. Oprah Winfrey - Oprah is a media mogul who has faced many obstacles on her path to success, including poverty and abuse as a child. Despite these challenges, she has always believed in herself and her ability to make a difference. She's used her platform to inspire and uplift others and has become a role model for millions around the world.

5. Thomas Edison. Determined resolution and a positive mindset carried him through 10,000 mistakes. He pondered the laws he already knew. He knew that current into metal makes a light. Too much oxygen causes the metal to burn too quickly. So he removed oxygen (created a vacuum in the bulb) and the first incandescent light was invented. Because he was successful there, the next invention idea he had worked on his first try!

6. Henry Ford – Henry Ford wasn't more intelligent or talented than anyone else, but he invented the first horseless carriage. There were tons of naysayers. He had to get a permit just to put it on the streets. But because he believed and didn't listen to the negative voices, the car became more available to people and changed the world.

These are just a few examples of individuals who have maintained positive mindsets in the face of adversity. Their stories remind us that we all have the power to choose our attitudes and outlooks, no matter what circumstances we face.

A positive mindset is a powerful tool that can help us to approach challenges with optimism, resilience, and creativity. By practicing positive self-talk, adopting a growth mindset, focusing on gratitude, and surrounding ourselves with positivity, we can cultivate a more positive outlook on life and achieve greater success, fulfillment, and happiness. Remember to approach challenges with a can-do attitude, embrace failure as an opportunity for growth, and focus on the good in every situation. With practice, you can develop a positive mindset and harness the power of positivity to transform your life.

Building Confidence Through Positive Self-Talk: How to Use Affirmations to Boost Your Self-Esteem

Self-confidence is essential for success in all areas of life, from personal relationships to professional endeavors. One of the most effective ways to build self-confidence is through positive self-talk. In this section, we will explore how positive self-talk can help you develop greater confidence and self-esteem.

Positive self-talk is the practice of using positive affirmations to improve your self-esteem and build confidence. It involves replacing negative thoughts and beliefs with positive, empowering statements that reinforce your self-worth and abilities.

Examples of Positive Affirmations

Here are some examples of positive affirmations that can help you build confidence:

1. I am capable of achieving my goals.

2. I am worthy of love and respect.

3. I have the power to overcome any challenge.

4. I am proud of who I am and what I have accomplished.

5. I am confident in my abilities and talents.

How Positive Self-Talk Can Build Confidence

1. It Reinforces Positive Beliefs: Positive affirmations can help you to reinforce positive beliefs about yourself, such as your worth, abilities, and potential. This can help you to develop greater self-confidence and a more positive self-image.

2. It Changes Your Mindset: By replacing negative self-talk with positive affirmations, you can change your mindset and develop a more optimistic, can-do attitude. This can help you to approach challenges with greater confidence and resilience.

3. It Boosts Motivation: Positive affirmations can help you to stay motivated and focused on your goals, by reminding you of your abilities and potential. This can help you to persevere in the face of obstacles and setbacks.

Tips for Practicing Positive Self-Talk

1. Identify Negative Self-Talk: Pay attention to the negative thoughts and beliefs that hold you back, and replace them with positive affirmations.

2. Use Specific, Positive Statements: Use specific, positive statements that reinforce your strengths and abilities, such as "I am a talented writer" or "I am an effective communicator."

3. Repeat Affirmations Daily: Repeat your affirmations daily, either in your mind or out loud, to reinforce positive beliefs and build confidence.

4. Visualize Success: Visualize yourself achieving your goals and succeeding in your endeavors, and use affirmations to reinforce your vision of success.

Positive self-talk is a powerful tool for building confidence and self-esteem. By using positive affirmations to reinforce positive beliefs, change your mindset, and boost motivation, you can develop greater confidence and achieve success in all areas of life. Remember to identify negative self-talk, use specific, positive statements, repeat affirmations daily, and visualize success to build your confidence and achieve your goals. With practice, you can transform your self-talk and build the self-confidence you need to succeed.

Improving Relationships with Positive Self-Talk: How to Use Affirmations to Foster Positive Connections

Our relationships with others are essential to our happiness and well-being. Positive self-talk can help us to improve our relationships by fostering positive connections and building stronger, more fulfilling relationships. In this section, we will explore how positive self-talk can help us to improve our relationships with others.

How Positive Self-Talk Can Improve Our Relationships

1. It Fosters Empathy: Positive affirmations can help us to develop greater empathy for others, by reminding us of our own strengths and weaknesses. This can help us to be more understanding and compassionate in our interactions with others.

2. It Builds Confidence: By replacing negative self-talk with positive affirmations, we can build greater confidence and self-esteem. This can help us to be more assertive and effective communicators in our relationships.

3. It Encourages Positive Communication: Positive affirmations can help us to approach our relationships with a more positive, open-minded attitude. This can encourage more positive communication and a deeper understanding between individuals.

Examples of Positive Affirmations

    1. I am an empathetic listener.

    2. I am patient and understanding.

    3. I communicate clearly and effectively.

    4. I am open-minded and non-judgmental.

    5. I am a positive influence on others.

Tips for Practicing Positive Self-Talk in Relationships

    1. Listen to Your Inner Voice: Pay attention to your inner voice and replace negative thoughts and beliefs with positive affirmations.

    2. Use Positive Language: Use positive language when communicating with others, such as "I appreciate you" or "I understand where you're coming from."

    3. Focus on Strengths: Focus on the strengths and positive qualities of others, rather than their weaknesses or faults.

    4. Practice Empathy: Put yourself in the other person's shoes and try to see things from their perspective.

Positive self-talk can help us to improve our relationships by fostering empathy, building confidence, and encouraging positive communication. By using positive affirmations to reinforce our self-worth and strengths, we can approach our relationships with a more positive, open-minded attitude. Remember to listen to your inner voice, use positive language, focus on strengths, and practice empathy to build stronger, more fulfilling relationships. With practice, you can transform your self-talk and improve your relationships with others.

Overcoming Obstacles with Positive Self-Talk

Life is full of obstacles, challenges, and setbacks. It is easy to get discouraged or feel defeated when we face difficult situations. However, one of the most powerful tools we have to overcome these obstacles is positive self-talk.

Positive self-talk is the practice of consciously directing our inner dialogue in a positive and constructive way. Instead of allowing negative thoughts and self-doubt to dominate our thinking, we intentionally choose to focus on the positive aspects of a situation and our own abilities to overcome it.

Here is an example of how positive self-talk can help us overcome obstacles:

Let's say you've just been passed over for a promotion at work. You feel disappointed and discouraged and start to doubt your own abilities. Negative thoughts start to creep in, like "I'm not good enough" or "I'll never get ahead."

However, with positive self-talk, you can reframe the situation and focus on the positive aspects. You might tell yourself, "This is a setback, but it's not the end of the world. I have a lot of strengths and skills that I can continue to develop. I'll keep working hard and striving to improve, and I know that eventually, I'll reach my goals."

By consciously directing your thoughts in a positive direction, you can shift your mindset from one of defeat to one of empowerment. Instead of feeling helpless and defeated, you feel motivated and energized to take action and overcome the obstacle in front of you.

Another example is challenging the thoughts in our heads. It is easy to feel like a failure if a situation doesn't go as hoped.

One day I presented at the Golden Hours Senior Center. The group was small - smaller than I had hoped. I gave my presentation and at the end, one lady came up to me and pretty much told me that my story didn't apply to her and wasn't helpful. That was all the feedback I got that day. So I began to think that experience was a failure because the group was so small and nobody really cared. Come to find out, there was another person in the room who was so touched by my story that she spent 45 minutes opening up to one of the leaders afterwards. Could I have known that at that moment? No. But could I have challenged my thoughts and used more positive self-talk? Yes.

Positive self-talk can be especially helpful in situations where we feel overwhelmed or unsure of ourselves. It can help us stay focused on our goals, build our confidence, and maintain a positive outlook, even when things don't go according to plan.

Of course, positive self-talk isn't a magic solution that will make all our problems disappear. Sometimes, we still need to take concrete actions to overcome obstacles, whether that means seeking out support from others, learning new skills, or making difficult choices.

By cultivating a positive mindset through self-talk, we can approach challenges with a greater sense of resilience, determination, and confidence. We can remind ourselves that we have the power to overcome obstacles and achieve our goals, even in the face of adversity.

Integrating Positive Self-Talk into Your Daily Life

Do you know why coaches and therapists give the advice they do? It is to give you knowledge and perspective to control your thoughts by managing your self-talk.

Positive self-talk can be a powerful tool for overcoming obstacles and achieving your goals. But how can you make it a regular part of your daily life? Here are some tips for integrating positive self-talk into your routine:

1. Start by becoming aware of your inner dialogue. Throughout the day, pay attention to the thoughts and self-talk that run through your mind. Are they mostly negative or positive? Are you harsh and critical with yourself, or do you offer yourself kindness and encouragement?

2. Reframe negative thoughts. When you notice negative self-talk, consciously reframe it in a positive way. For example, if you catch yourself thinking, "I'm not good enough," try changing it to "I'm doing the best I can, and I can learn and improve over time."

3. Use affirmations. Affirmations are short, positive statements that you repeat to yourself to reinforce positive beliefs and attitudes. Choose a few affirmations that resonate with you, such as "I am capable and strong," "I trust myself to make good decisions," or "I am worthy of love and respect." Repeat them to yourself throughout the day, or write them down and place them somewhere you'll see them frequently.

4. Celebrate your successes. When you achieve a goal or make progress toward something you've been working on, take a moment to acknowledge and celebrate your success. Offer yourself positive self-talk, such as "I'm proud of myself for accomplishing this," or "I worked hard and it paid off."

Celebrating first downs

In American Football, the ultimate objective is to score more points than your opponent. This can be done mainly through touchdowns or field goals. Each team has four chances, known as "downs", to move the ball 10 yards forward. After achieving this ten-yard mark, the team will gain an additional four "downs" or attempts at furthering their progress toward a touchdown.

When a football team achieves the goal of a first down, the audience erupts in cheers! But why? No points have been scored yet so what is there to celebrate? The answer is progress:

> Every first down brings the team 10 yards closer to the end zone and that is worth celebrating!

If no one cared about first downs, then football would be much different.

What are your first downs? How do you celebrate your progress along the way?

5. Practice self-compassion. It's important to be kind and compassionate with yourself, especially when things don't go according to plan. When you make a mistake or face a setback, offer yourself words of comfort and understanding, such as "It's okay to make mistakes, I can learn from this and do better next time."

6. Surround yourself with positivity. Surrounding yourself with positive people, environments, and media can help reinforce positive self-talk. Seek out uplifting books, podcasts, and social media accounts that inspire and motivate you, and spend time with friends and family who support and encourage you.

By integrating positive self-talk into your daily routine, you can cultivate a more positive mindset, boost your confidence and resilience, and become better equipped to handle life's challenges. With practice, positive self-talk can become a habit, helping you to approach each day with a greater sense of positivity, purpose, and joy.

Conclusion

Much is determined during the conversations you have in your mind. How do you control or change those?

Stand guard at the door of your mind.

What changes your mind? Frequency and intensity of thoughts or ideas. This is why marketing works. If you can't be intense, be frequent.

Remember how you keep seeing that particular ad? You don't think much of it when it shows up but you have seen it so many times that now you think there must be something to it so you give it more attention. That is frequency.

Pay attention to the voice you repeatedly listen to. If you have a habit of listening to the negative voice, recognize it, cast it out, and flip it to a positive one! Use the principle of frequency to your benefit. Frequently listen to the positive voice. Turn that volume up!

Positive self-talk is a powerful tool that can help you overcome obstacles, achieve your goals, and cultivate a more positive mindset. By becoming more aware of your inner dialogue and consciously reframing negative thoughts into positive ones, you can create a more empowering and supportive self-talk that can help you navigate life's challenges with greater resilience and optimism.

If you're ready to take your positive self-talk to the next level, here are some next steps you can take:

1. Set intentions: Identify specific areas of your life where you want to cultivate more positive self-talk. This could be related to your relationships, career, health, or personal growth.

2. Practice regularly: Like any skill, positive self-talk requires practice and repetition. Incorporate positive self-talk into your daily routine, and make it a habit.

3. Use positive affirmations: Choose a few affirmations that resonate with you and repeat them to yourself regularly.

4. Surround yourself with positivity: Seek out people, environments, and media that reinforce positive self-talk. Spend time with supportive friends and family, and seek out uplifting books, podcasts, and social media accounts.

5. Be patient and persistent: Changing your self-talk habits takes time and effort. Be patient with yourself, and don't give up if you don't see immediate results. With persistence and dedication, positive self-talk can become a natural part of your daily life.

Remember, positive self-talk is a journey, not a destination. It requires ongoing effort and attention to cultivate a more positive and empowering mindset. By taking small steps every day and making positive self-talk a habit, you can create a more fulfilling and joyful life, and achieve the success and happiness you desire.

Summary of Chapter 7

- Learn to observe the thoughts in your head before believing them at face value.

- Learn to recognize the voices in your head so you can cast out the devil.

- Changing how you talk to yourself can make a huge difference in your life.

Questions for Application:

- Can you recall a recent instance where you engaged in negative self-talk? How did it affect your behavior?

- What positive affirmations or statements can you use to counteract negative self-talk and reinforce a healthier self-concept?

- How can your accountability partner help you with this?

Chapter 8 - Emotions: How Do You Feel About Yourself?

> *"We are not creatures of logic. We are creatures of emotion. Our logic is like a birch-bark canoe tossed about on a deep, dark, stormy sea of emotion."*
>
> Dale Carnegie

How do I feel?

Understanding emotions

"Learning about emotions teaches you the ability to control impulses, delay gratification, motivate yourself, read other people's social cues, and cope with life's ups and downs."
John M Gottman

Clarity and intelligence bring light and power.

Think about what this means.

Clarity means you can more clearly see something. That is what light does.

Intelligence is power. Why? The more you understand, the more options you have to choose. When you have options to choose from, you have more power over your future.

The same applies to emotions. When you gain clarity over your emotions, you can see them more clearly because of the light you are shining on them. Where there is light there can be no darkness. The more you understand your emotions, the more options you have to choose - to choose what you will do with those emotions, how you will react, and who you will become.

Have you ever seen the Disney/Pixar movie "Inside Out"?

The story is about an 11-year-old girl named Riley. Riley lives a happy life with her parents and is really good at hockey. The movie depicts five emotions in Riley's head: Joy, Sadness, Anger, Disgust, and Fear. If any of the emotions touch the controls, she feels that emotion. Joy is pretty much in charge and tries to keep everyone happy.

All of a sudden, Riley and her family have to leave their happy life and move to a new state. Although she tries to stay happy, the house is not what she expected, the moving truck is days late, and her parents don't have time to play hockey around the house with her like they used to. Sadness begins to get involved, but Joy does all she can to keep her out of it.

Riley went to her new school and as she was introducing herself, she told everyone how she missed her old house and she began to cry in front of everyone. Because she felt Sadness had embarrassed her, she and Joy began to try to put Sadness into a corner.

Finally, she tried out for the hockey team. This was normally her outlet where she could enjoy what she was good at. But because she wasn't emotionally sound, (Joy and Sadness were fighting and Anger, Fear, and Disgust didn't know what to do) she didn't play well.

Joy and Sadness ended up being sucked out of the control room. Because only Anger, Fear, and Disgust were left, she was angry, short, and rude to her parents. She didn't like how she felt and thought the only solution was to go back to her old home where everything was good and happy.

Notice two principles here.

> 1. Because she tried to turn off Sadness, she also turned off its complimentary emotion: Joy.

> "We cannot selectively numb emotions, when we numb the painful emotions, we also numb the positive emotions."
>
> Brene Brown

2. Because she had unresolved emotions (she hadn't talked to anyone or allowed the emotions to flow) her brain looked for something to make her feel better. Her coping mechanism that usually worked was hockey. Because that didn't work, she got even more frustrated. That "solution" was to go home to her old "normal." What the brain doesn't realize is that the "old normal" doesn't exist anymore.

Here is when, because of her emotional pain (or unresolved emotions) she decides to do something that goes against her values. The brain wants relief so badly that it starts to ignore the values it normally cares so much about. She decided to steal her mom's credit card so she could buy a bus ticket home. During this moment, she could still change her mind, truly think about what she was doing, and decide to talk to someone about what she was feeling. But she let the emotions control her and she stole the credit card. She was scared but left in a huff (using anger as a motivator and also as a shield for her fear). She bought the bus ticket and boarded the bus. After a few minutes, her logical side of the brain caught up to her and she thought, "What am I doing? I will be all alone back home. My parents won't be there. How will I take care of myself? This isn't the best idea after all."

She got off the bus and headed home. She opened the front door and found her parents in a nervous state because they didn't know where their daughter was and they had been calling all over town.

Here are two important principles to understand at this moment:

1. Riley is very scared and vulnerable right now. What happens next will be pivotal in what she learns about how to resolve her emotions.

2. The parents are scared. Like anyone, fear can cause us to lash out (fight). This means the parents could look at the daughter and say, "Where the heck have you been!? Don't you realize we have been looking all over for you? It is late, past your curfew, etc... YOU STOLE THE CREDIT CARD?!?!? How could you? " Etc.

Realize what would have happened if the parents reacted this way. Riley would have learned that the parents don't care about what she is going through. She would think they don't understand. All they do is make her feel worse and she needs to get away from them as soon as possible.

Then the parents wonder why the daughter never opens up to them anymore.

Here is what really happened.

The parents saw Riley with her head down. They took compassion on her and threw their arms around her in a hug and said they were so glad she was home safe. Riley, who was scared, vulnerable, and not sure what to do, now felt safe enough to cry. Crying made the parents care for her even more and therefore turned this memory into a positive one of closeness. Crying (Sadness) allowed Joy back into her life.

And so we learn another important lesson: The parents saw her as the daughter they loved (identity) first. Doing so allowed them to acknowledge her emotions as a person.

Addressing the emotional needs first allows for connection and healing. Addressing the behavior first brings separation and judgment.

This being said, you may ask, "How then do we teach people what is wrong and right? Do we just allow any behavior because the person is emotional?"

No. We can and should set limits on behaviors. But realize the importance of addressing the emotions in conjunction with the teaching behavior. The world of today focuses too much on behavior without addressing emotions. Because of this, people will conform their behavior but distance themselves emotionally to the point that there will be conflict, separation, or apathy in the relationship.

People first need to understand they are not the problem. There is no need to feel ashamed of how they feel. They are not the only ones who feel that way - they are not alone.

Don't set limits on emotion—set standards for the behavior. Help them regulate their feelings, find appropriate outlets, and solve problems.

What do you learn from this story?

When Riley tried to remove Sadness from her life she also lost Joy. That left only Anger, Fear, and Disgust. Think about your life. Do you feel one of these emotions more than the other? If so, maybe you need to take some time to allow Sadness and Joy back into your life.

During times of isolation, it is even more important to know how to understand and acknowledge your emotions. Without this knowledge, emotions such as fear, anger, and sadness can overwhelm you.

Sometimes, because of how we were raised, when people express emotions we either jump to conclusions (in an effort to resolve them) or we expect a catastrophe.

Neither of these have to be true. Emotions are a normal part of life. If we see them as the brain trying to send us a message, we can pause and try to understand that message so we can move on without having to find ways to cope with or deny them.

There are no good or bad emotions - just good and bad ways of expressing them. You can control your behavior. It is done by properly managing your emotions.

If your emotions aren't handled, they can lead to drastic and unproductive behavior.

When Riley was emotionally overwhelmed, she experienced a "so what" moment. "So what? It doesn't matter anyway. Nobody really cares and I just want to feel better so I am going to take this into my own hands."

Once she left home, she could have had the thought, "I can never go back home now. Look what I've done." This is why when people behave in drastic ways, they feel they can never come back.

When Riley got back home, her body language was sad and a little scared. She showed us that it feels good to have the courage to express your feelings to someone who can help. It didn't change the fact that she moved, but she dealt with the emotions so she could accept the event. You can't change what happened, but you can move on from it by experiencing your emotions.

Have you ever had a time where you lashed out in anger, fear, or disgust? Maybe you did so because you didn't know what else to do. Then you were ashamed and began to hate yourself for it. It caused a downward spiral.

Rather than get mad at someone who does this, we should realize what is really happening and help them through their emotions. Love them. This still applies if we are talking about you.

Think of what happened to Riley that caused all of this. She moved. Things were not what she expected. She went to a new school and felt embarrassed in front of everyone because she cried on her first day. She messed up at the one thing she was good at – hockey. She didn't understand why all this was happening and couldn't really talk to her parents about it because she knew they wanted her to be her normal happy self. She didn't want to bother them with her feelings. Her dad was busy and her mom just wanted to be positive.

She was different at the dinner table. She didn't want to talk about it and she wasn't ready to talk about it because she didn't even know what was going on yet. She acted out in anger, fear, and disgust.

She wanted to do something to make her feel better. So she stole her mom's credit card to buy a bus ticket back to Minnesota. This whole experience could have led to feelings of shame.

How do you deal with this as a caring onlooker?

Realize that she is hurting emotionally. Validate her feelings first and then set barriers on behavior. Stealing is never ok. She should talk to someone. But make sure you address why she stole in the first place so she can learn that she doesn't need to go there ever again.

Learning the Language of Emotion

I know a guy who speaks three languages fluently and says he will learn a fourth in less than a year. I was very impressed and thought of all he could do with the ability to speak four different languages.

Then I thought, "What about the language of Emotion? How many people are fluent in that? Imagine what clearer communication we could have if we spoke fluent Emotion?"

Learning the language of Emotion can be done the same way as learning any language. You begin by believing you can do it and by being patient with yourself. Begin to increase your vocabulary. Surround yourself with opportunities to practice - and practice as often as possible.

If you are worried about making mistakes or feeling embarrassed, let me share a personal story. I studied Spanish in high school. I was a good student and wasn't worried about learning the language, but I did fear making a mistake in front of someone. That fear caused me not to speak the language out loud very much with others unless I was very sure of myself. On the other hand, I had a friend who would just try to speak Spanish all the time. He made so many mistakes it was embarrassing! But a few months later I realized that although I understood the rules of Spanish really well, my friend spoke better Spanish than I did.

I learned an important lesson. When learning something new, you are going to make mistakes. It is pretty much guaranteed. In fact, let's say that you are guaranteed to make 10,000 mistakes before you become fluent in the language. Do you want to avoid making those mistakes and thus take years to become fluent or do you want to get them over with as soon as possible so you can quickly speak the language and connect to the people around you? It is your choice!

Speaking the language of Emotion applies both when understanding what is going on inside yourself as well as when you are trying to connect with others.

If you are in the habit of ignoring your emotions, then you become quite closed off. Emotions are how we connect to others. If you don't believe me, think of Spock from Star Trek. The Vulcans don't truly connect to others because they are purely logical. Listening to your emotions does require that you be open and vulnerable, but that also makes you approachable.

We would have much deeper connections and relationships if we all learned to speak the language of Emotion.

What are emotions telling me?

8 Basic Emotions
And the purpose of each one

- **Anger** — To fight against problems
- **Fear** — To protect us from danger
- **Anticipation** — To look forward and plan
- **Surprise** — To focus us on new situations
- **Joy** — To remind us what's important
- **Sadness** — To connect us with those we love
- **Trust** — To connect with people who help
- **Disgust** — To reject what is unhealthy

Happiness is when your basic human needs are being met and you focus on what you have. This can be described as calm, peaceful, joyful, and elated.

Sadness is when we experience some form of loss.

Anger makes us protect or fight for something. It can highlight what is truly important to us.

Some people fear anger and sadness will stay with you your whole life. Those who live with unending sadness have learned to hate it.

The reason they stay so long is because they have never been fully addressed in the first place. It is experiencing them, not ignoring them, that gets them to give way to joy.

Confidence is when we see ourselves and have enough certainty to be able to focus on other people.

Pride is when we see ourselves and we want to show everyone else how we are better than them.

Shame is when we see ourselves and we don't want anyone else to see what we see.

Guilt and Shame

Guilt is about the behavior. Shame is about the person.

Guilt is: You made a mistake. Shame is: You are a mistake.

Separating character from behavior is crucial.

Guilt causes you to want to change.

Shame causes you to self-medicate in ways that are harmful. You may feel better in the moment but you feel worse afterwards and it leads to a spiral.

Brene Brown tells us that three things grow shame: Silence, Secrecy, and Judgment.

You break that by doing the opposite. Speak, Share, Connect.

Shame's antidote is empathy. How it is administered is through talking, sharing, and connecting.

We don't often talk about things like shame because we don't want to feel it and we don't like how we feel when we talk about it. If we do, we think there must be something wrong with us.

What does shame make you do? Isolate. Not talk to anyone. Want to hurt yourself. Think the world would be better without you.

Your emotions are speaking to you all the time but how often do you actually listen? Have you practiced receiving and understanding the message? Or do you treat your emotions like an annoying child and just hope they go away?

Emotions are simply the brain's way of trying to send us a message. We should learn to interpret the message before denying the messenger.

If you don't resolve your emotions, they will stick with you until the message coming from your body is delivered.

Think of it, if someone misunderstands excitement as anxiety, that person becomes afraid of their future and turns to medicine.

Imagine something that you are looking forward to but also makes you a little anxious. Think of the anxiety. Where do you feel it? In your stomach? Now think of the excitement. Where do you feel it? Butterflies in the stomach? Both are felt in the stomach! Anxiety and excitement are very related emotions - in fact, they are two sides of the same coin. You can be excited about something because it is important to you and you look forward to what can come when it goes well. You can also be nervous because it is important to you and you worry about what can come if it doesn't go well. The key is to focus on what you are excited about and prepare for that, rather than get stuck in fear and focus on all that can go wrong.

It helps to understand your emotions so you don't misinterpret the message.

Anxiety and perfectionism are very related. They both worry about the future.

Depression is more worried about what happened in the past and therefore dampens your excitement for the future.

You are not your emotions. Sometimes we think of depression and anxiety as extremes that are incurable. We all experience depression and anxiety at times but that does not make you "depressed" or "anxious." You may be experiencing those feelings, but they don't define you.

Fear is meant to keep us safe—fight, flight, freeze, or fawn. It is an emotion in the present when you focus on what you can't control in the future.

Faith is focusing on what you can control in the future. Faith brings confidence. Why? Because you are focusing on what you can control and faith brings action, which adds to your confidence as you begin to progress. Faith is also trusting in a higher power that can get you through this situation.

If you are nervous, anxious, or afraid, it is probably because you don't know how something will turn out. You are afraid of the unknown. Therefore, all you have to do is learn something or gain some knowledge about the subject. Intelligence brings light and understanding. Light dispels darkness and fear. So in scary or stressful times, ask yourself, "What do I know? What else can I find out?" Then take that small step forward.

For example, it is said that one of the most common fears is the fear of public speaking. Why is that? Is a bear going to pop out of nowhere and eat you for lunch as you are switching through slides? Is a swarm of bees going to fly up your nose as you take your first breath? No! You are afraid of how the audience will react. You are afraid they won't like what you say or that you just look and sound silly.

See how all of these examples are focusing on something in the future that you can't control? So what is the opposite? Focus on what you can control. You don't control how the audience will react, but you can control how much you care about the audience and how often you use their names. You don't control whether they will like your speech or not, but you do control how you can tell a story that is perfect for Sally because you had a brief conversation with her prior to your speech.

You can apply this to dating and relationships as well. You may be terrified just thinking about dating. Maybe you struggle to ask someone out because of your fear. Fear of what? Fear of what you can't control in the future: What if she says no? What if I get embarrassed? What if I stutter? What if...?

What is the opposite? You don't control how she will react, but you can control your actions by walking up to her, giving your best smile, and confidently asking her name. Then you can ask the simple words of "Will you go out with me?"

I know some of you may be reading this and your brain will sprint forward after this last line and start to think, "I can't do that! What if she says 'no'? I will be so embarrassed, etc." Remember, focus on what you can control and take those small steps forward. Even if the girl says "no" at least you asked her out! Now you don't have to worry or be anxious thinking about whether or not you should approach her. You already did and you survived! Celebrate the fact that you tried and make a plan for next time. It becomes easier the more you do it.

Confidence comes from a correct understanding of something - primarily of who you are.

If you tell someone they just need more confidence, that tells them they don't have it. How are they supposed to gain it when you are blatantly pointing out what they lack? The better way is to give them confidence by complimenting them or believing in them.

Lack of self-confidence comes from two places: the future and the past.

It comes from the future because you may be thinking, "I want to do ____ but I am nowhere near where I think I should be, therefore I am just not cut out for this."

It comes from the past when we focus on past failures. "I have tried and tried already but it just didn't work – therefore it will never work."

This is focusing on what you lack.

Self-confidence comes from knowing you are enough.

My clients often tell me that I help them feel a lot more confident. Many of my clients are leaders and entrepreneurs. They are doing great things. Many things are working but they seriously doubt themselves. They are very self-critical.

As we talk, I discover how they are talking to themselves. It is usually with words like, "How come I can't do better than this? Why isn't this working? Why can't I be more confident? Why can't I _____?"

You notice that the whys are in the negative and there are a lot of "can'ts" there. When they are asking themselves these questions, it is no wonder they feel discouraged! No wonder they worry they aren't good enough to be in their current position. No wonder they experience imposter syndrome or lack confidence!

When we work together we simply shine a light on those thoughts. We take them from the subconscious (you know, the thoughts you don't realize you have every day until someone points them out to you) and use the power of thought to turn them into powerful thoughts. We rephrase things. Instead of "How come I can't do better than this?" we change it to, "What have I done well lately? What is working? What can I celebrate today?" Then their focus changes and they take their mental faculties out of the pit they have been wallowing in and they start to remember things and feel better.

I realize that people may be so far removed from this habit that it is a struggle to think of positive things. I experienced this myself in therapy. My therapist asked me to name five positive memories in the past ten years. I struggled to think of them because I had discounted them all. I was so deep in my pain and negative self-talk that I discounted every good thing I had done. Some of my clients experience a similar thing but not on such a deep level (many of my clients have also met with a therapist before working with me). Regardless, I encourage them and help them remember things worth celebrating. We focus on the fact that they and their accomplishments are worth celebrating. When their mind catches hold of this fact, a spark ignites in their eyes. You see a change in their demeanor because it feels good! They know this is true and it feels great to be given permission to celebrate those things!

One specific client, we'll call her Polly, would have a habit of finishing a project or task and then immediately moving on to thinking about the next task. She was always in a cycle of "What is next and what else needs to happen?" But she never acknowledged her progress! Without that acknowledgment and celebration, her mind never learned the confidence from progress so she was in a state where she felt she had to be the hero for everyone. She wanted to live up to her Director title and be able to help everyone. Because she thought this, she felt she could never turn off from work. She never took time for herself. She always said yes. She never felt prepared enough during meetings or in conversations.

She was a high achiever - very capable, successful, and smart. Through our sessions, she developed a habit of reflecting on what was working in her life. Because she did this and learned to challenge negative thinking, she mastered her thoughts and ended up scheduling and honoring time for herself on her calendar each day. She finally took a vacation! She showed up confidently to meetings. She was still able to be a high achiever and high performer, but she was so much happier!

As you think into the future in a state of preparation (not anxiety), you show up in confidence. How do you do that? Again, it comes down to what questions you ask yourself and what thoughts you allow to run through your mind. Most people, when it comes to the future, have no plan, and their heads are filled with "what if", "who knows", and "it doesn't matter." No wonder they fear the future! But if you can face the future with purpose and a set mind you will see it differently.

For example, Polly was preparing for a meeting. She was nervous about the meeting because she felt she wasn't prepared with the numbers, she didn't know how to respond to the team members when they asked questions, and she didn't have time to have a meeting to plan another meeting. As we talked, we challenged those thoughts. *Was she prepared with the numbers?* Yes. Did she have all the numbers she could? If so, why was she nervous? If not, could she get more numbers before the meeting?

She didn't know how to respond to the team members. What does that mean? Why did she think that? She brought up experiences from the past. We then considered possible responses to questions. She realized that even in the worst-case scenario if she had all the wrong data, she could have a plan on what to do in that case. She would know what data was needed. She would know what questions to ask in response. She would be grateful for the feedback. She cut through her fears and realized these people weren't out to get her and they didn't doubt her ability in her role. They were all there trying to accomplish the same thing and they just wanted communication.

On the other hand, if she discovered they had enough data, she could make the executive decision to proceed with their plan. When she caught hold of this idea, you could see her face light up. She didn't realize that was a possibility! She hated feeling powerless and thinking she didn't know how to progress past this meeting. When she saw a new possibility, she re-engaged her executive mind and planned the rest of the meeting and it went as she desired.

Confidence comes when you challenge your negative thoughts and stand in what you know to be true.

Loneliness

Have you ever been in a room full of people and yet felt lonely?

Have you ever found it easier to "be in charge" or "be busy" than to interact with people?

As the president of my college choir, I had a lot of responsibilities. My days were spent planning meetings and events, organizing assignments, and assigning duties to each member. I put all my energy into serving others, but that left me little time to truly connect with people. At these events, everyone knew my name and smiled when they saw me, yet despite this façade of popularity, I felt like an outsider. There was a loneliness inside me, hidden beneath the smile on my face as I dutifully did my job.

Although I didn't like feeling this way, it became a protection for anxiety when in groups. Rather than go through the awkwardness of trying to talk to others, I would just look for ways to be helpful and look busy. That way I was around people but didn't have to be embarrassed. That avoided the anxiety but it did nothing for loneliness.

Many of my clients come to me feeling alone. You wouldn't know it at first because they seem very involved or very happy. But they have been isolating themselves emotionally for quite some time. Whether it is because they are a leader (leadership can be lonely) or because they are building something new and haven't built a team yet, they have been going at it alone.

They have tried different coping mechanisms but none of them have worked.

Many times they recharge while alone or they spend a lot of their time stuck in their own head.

Loneliness can cause you to do things against your values. You long for connection and therefore may compromise your values to fit in or to get someone to like you.

Anger

Do you think it is not okay to get angry? Do you think you aren't allowed to feel that way? Emotions are part of life. If you can learn to experience them early, you can catch them while they are at a low level.

Those who have lived with unbridled anger have learned to run from it. Or they have turned to violence to protect themselves or feel heard.

Sometimes it helps to reflect on how you were raised and see how it has affected your ability to face emotions. This experience is not to place blame on your parents but to understand and take responsibility for where you are today. That is when you gain the power to do something about it.

Here is an example from a client of mine.

This client came to me with a history of depression and suicidal ideations. After getting to know her, I learned that she grew up with a father who drank and could be violent at times. It was natural for this client to be scared.

After years of living in this fear, it became hard to separate herself from it. In other words, she had begun to accept it as just a part of life. She learned to protect herself with anger. But she directed that anger at herself. She didn't want to show emotions because that was considered a "weakness." She hid her emotions and therefore got angry at herself whenever she felt something. Because she never expressed her emotions, she became depressed. The overwhelming feeling of unresolved and unexpressed emotions caused her to consider suicide.

On the outside, she looked like the happiest and nicest girl you would ever meet. But on the inside, she was always angry and hiding fear and sadness.

Because she had suppressed her emotions for so many years, she didn't trust her feelings. She was extremely worried about disappointing people. She didn't know how to act around others. This added to the internal feelings but she kept pushing them down with anger.

When she came to me, I could have focused on behavior: You need to love your dad. You need to practice being real with people, etc.

If I had begun with this, she would have stopped coming to me because she would still have her unresolved emotions and they would get in the way of achieving these different behaviors.

So I worked with her and helped her understand and acknowledge her emotions.

While working with her, I learned some other stories she had begun to tell herself because of the unresolved emotions she was carrying around. She wondered why her family situation wasn't perfect or ideal. She was afraid that God didn't love her. She wondered why it seemed He didn't answer her prayers. She distanced herself from Him.

Many people leave God because they are angry at Him. If they could understand why and that maybe they were just hiding their fear, they wouldn't leave their Father who could take away the pain.

Understand your emotions so you don't leave God. Then continue to trust in Him while studying the scriptures and praying.

As I helped her understand and acknowledge her emotions, she was open to the idea of letting God back into her life.

I helped her know that it is okay to feel and to have different emotions. It is okay to cry, to be upset, to love, to feel embarrassed, etc. As she felt more and more permission to feel, she was ready to understand what she was covering with her anger.

Anger is a secondary emotion and often hides fear, sadness, or pain. This client was hiding her fear of being vulnerable, of getting hurt, of disappointing someone, of not being good enough.

When she understood all of this and acknowledged the truth behind the anger, she began to feel more control over her anger. She began to realize that, while it is not a problem to experience anger, she doesn't need to be controlled by it, and she can choose when and how she will react to anger.

What were the results of this? She was much more confident in herself. She believed in herself. She learned to stand on her own two feet and follow her dreams. She overcame her fears, started a business to follow her passion, and even found and married the love of her life!

Do you see how the positive results she wanted came as a result of resolving her emotions?

If your boss is always angry, especially when you bring up bad news, how will you react? Will you continue to make efforts to talk to him (or her) if you know they will just get angry?

What about a parent? Do you think a close bond can be formed if the parent is always angry and frustrated at the child?

No. Why? Anger from a person in authority is often seen as an attack. What is your natural reaction when you feel attacked? You either fight back or you run and hide. The former isn't very feasible because it will destroy your relationship and could get you fired or kicked out of the home. The latter is more common but it can look different with different people. Some people literally leave their homes or workplaces because they are tired of the anger directed at them. Others don't physically run, but they are mentally gone. They are now in a mode where they just need to do the very minimum to protect themselves. And people wonder why others get so closed off sometimes...

In one of my jobs, my boss had a cousin who worked for him. As time progressed, the cousin wasn't meeting expectations and my boss asked me to look for his replacement.

We discussed the transition details and agreed that he would speak to his cousin before the arrival of the new employee. I waited patiently to hear back from my boss on when this would happen, but time passed and the last day before the replacement was due came without any communication. To avoid future embarrassment and because other steps relied on the completion of this one, I made an executive decision and mentioned the transition in our meeting.

My boss exploded and asked, "What is your problem?!?"

He was furious with me for bringing it up in the meeting.

I was embarrassed because I tried my best to not do anything wrong. I was confused because I was just trying to do what he asked me to and this was the only way I knew how.

From my perspective, I didn't think the anger was warranted because it was something we had talked about and he hadn't done his part. I could have gotten angry back or tried to just brush it off (hide and pretend it never happened).

But because of what I knew about the emotion of anger, I asked myself, "If anger often hides fear, is it possible my boss is hiding fear right now?"

Well, he hadn't spoken to his cousin yet and I had mentioned his replacement in his presence. My boss always avoided tough conversations like this and was probably not ready for the potential embarrassment with his cousin. He could have been afraid of what would happen when the cousin found out (especially because it might affect family parties from now on).

So what came off as my boss getting angry at me for doing my best to help the company hire a powerful replacement and avoiding embarrassment when nothing was ready on that person's first day, may have actually been him hiding his fear and embarrassment. This understanding was pivotal for me. It didn't justify his anger or ignore the fact that I was hurt and embarrassed in front of everyone. But it did help me not turn to anger and revenge for something I could label as "unjust."

I have since learned that others' behavior towards you is often a reflection of what is going on inside them. Here is where the phrase "It's not you, it's me" actually applies.

When someone expresses anger or communicates a complaint or criticism, the best course of action would be to not get defensive but to think of what the other person is feeling. Why are they making that comment? Address that and the problem is solved.

> *"If you're like most people, you were not raised with the ability to understand or deal with your negative emotions appropriately. Much of that is because we just haven't known that our feelings have a purpose or that we have a lot of control over them.*
>
> *The result is that we might become overwhelmed by a negative emotion or we may try to deny it.*
>
> *Other times you may start feeling an emotion but you interrupt the experience without honoring the emotion. This can be through self-medicating, jumping into other feelings, numbing yourself, or changing the subject altogether because you don't like how you feel and want it to stop.*
>
> *The result is emotional denial and it will frequently lead to the creation of a trapped emotion. This is the emotional equivalent of sweeping dirt under the rug."*
> The Emotion Code

Don't disapprove of emotions. Too many people think they "can't" be sad or angry so they try to bury the emotion. What that really does is bottle it until it shows up later in an even less desirable way.

Many people think they can't show emotion. They have to be strong for their family and friends. Really? Aren't your family and friends the ones that are often most ready to help you? And if they can't help you, they will be willing to connect you with someone who can.

If you are afraid of showing emotions it is usually because of one of a few reasons. 1. You are worried about what other people will think. 2. You are afraid the emotions will control you and you will do something you regret. 3. You downplay the emotion saying "It's fine. I'm fine. It's no big deal."

Would you agree that we all would prefer to always feel happy? Isn't that just a comfortable feeling to have? No worries? Just peace and calm and feeling good.

I would argue that unless you know how to choose to be happy, you haven't learned to control your emotions yet. Let's say happiness is a natural state. If you are out of that state, it is because something has happened and you haven't resolved it yet so you can return to your natural state. So simply wishing that you were happy again isn't going to cut it.

Emotions that "drag you down" are unpleasant and can be hard to deal with. But these are a natural part of life and we can learn to properly resolve them and return to our natural state of happiness.

Understanding your emotions empowers you to change your inner dialogue. You no longer wonder why you cannot change your behavior, why you always get the results that you don't want, and why it affects people the way it does. You no longer have to wonder why you feel the way you do!

Emotion logs can be helpful for people who feel scared or anxious about their own emotional responses. John Gottman helps us understand why:

> "The process of labeling an emotion and writing about it can help you define and contain your feelings. Emotions that once seemed mysterious and uncontrollable suddenly take on boundaries and limits. Our feelings become more manageable and they're not as frightening anymore."

I love the book series "The SoulKeepers" by GP Ching. I will include a few excerpts here and then break them down to illustrate what is happening.

Malini, one of the main girls in the story, was feeling lost because she didn't fully understand her role in the group. She wanted to be strong and helpful but she felt lost and confused.

"With both of them staring after her, she left, feeling drained of everything but her will to get beyond this. She stomped to her car and slipped behind the wheel, but didn't start the engine. Instead, she allowed the tinted windows to shield her from the outside world and permitted herself to feel what she couldn't in front of [them].

The tears came then. A few slipping down her cheeks before growing into face-drenching sobs. There was a hole inside of her. The binding that held her together had cracked and the stuff she'd always counted on to glue her pieces back in place was leaking uselessly into her bloodstream.

'Tell me what I'm supposed to do,' she screamed to Heaven. It wasn't a prayer. It was a tantrum. Her fists hit the steering wheel in a rage that seemed to blossom from the inside out. 'What am I supposed to be?' The questions bounced off the windshield. 'What's the big secret?' Her fists pounded hard enough to leave bruises. 'If you want me for your team of Soulkeepers, bring me on, but stop messing with my life.'"

Can you relate to any of this? She tried to be strong in front of her friends and family. She "couldn't" feel in front of her friends. Because she had held her emotions in for so long, she finally burst.

Thankfully, she burst in a productive way. She didn't hurt anyone. She opened up to someone who could help.

Soon after releasing her emotions (through crying, releasing energy, and talking about her feelings), she felt much better and was able to move on in a much better way. She felt more sure of herself.

Malini later discovered her role in the SoulKeepers group. But she also discovered that someone could have helped her all this time.

"All this time I've been tortured wondering what I was, if there was even a name for it, and you two knew and let me go on like that..."

Someone who doesn't know how to name their emotions can feel like Malini. They feel confused, lost, and powerless. Learning to give a name to what you are feeling gives you power over them. Otherwise, your brain goes crazy because of the unknowns.

There was an episode of Brain Games about this. The volunteer was blindfolded and plunged into total darkness, their body strapped to a chair like a helpless puppet. With unnerving anticipation, they felt slimy scales brush over their feet, heard the deafening flapping of leather wings echoing in their ear, and felt the tiny whiskers of rats scurry across their toes. Fear filled every inch of their being as they imagined what was in the room with them.

The truth was that the "snake" was a rubber tube, the "bat" was just some plastic, and the "rats" were props. Knowing the truth, (having clarity and intelligence on what it actually was) dispelled the volunteer's fear.

Try this for yourself. Go into a dark, unfamiliar room. All the noises, feelings, and experiences may begin to give you feelings of confusion and powerlessness. But as soon as you understand what they are (by turning the light on and observing what is actually there), your fear will disappear.

What do you think is the most difficult part when it comes to emotions?

I surveyed a group of over 200 young adults and asked them "What do you think is the most difficult part when it comes to emotions?" I will include some of the most common responses and I will comment on a few. Can you relate to any of them?

Allowing yourself to feel and knowing it is ok to feel

This deals with the fear of the unknown (not being experienced with emotions and possibly linking the expression of that emotion to an experience in the past that didn't go very well)

Giving yourself permission to feel is one of the most important steps to resolving your emotions.

Letting the emotions exist (not blocking emotions)

Again, this comes down to either inexperience with emotions or a link to a past, negative experience with allowing emotions to exist. The emotion will not hurt you.

Not letting them control you

Of course, you don't want to be controlled by any emotion. You don't want to do anything you would regret or be embarrassed by your behavior. The more aware of your emotions you become, the more control you will have over them.

Managing the intensity of emotions

This is a sign of misunderstanding how to resolve emotions. If you try to manage the intensity of the emotion, you are trying to ignore and deny part of it. The true solution is to give yourself space and permission to fully experience the emotion so that it can be resolved and leave your body. A good thing to keep in mind is to resolve the emotion while it is small rather than letting it build until it is ready to explode. (See section on emotional stacking)

Discerning emotions (knowing which ones you are feeling)

This one is important because it is linked to the feeling of control over your emotions. Once you put a name to an emotion, you will feel more control over it.

You can do a simple internet search for "emotion wheel" or "emotion chart" and find many examples that will help expand your vocabulary for emotions. You can then find which emotion most closely fits what you are feeling.

If you need further help, that is where a professional coach or therapist can help you.

Acknowledging emotions

To acknowledge an emotion is to call it by name, hear its message, and honor its existence. Once you do so, it can leave because it has finished its job.

Separate thoughts from feelings

Thoughts and feelings are linked to one another. I don't believe it is productive to try to separate (disconnect) thoughts from feelings. But if the connotation is to discern thoughts from feelings, that can be very valuable because that is engaging the logical mind to regain control over the emotional side of the brain. Being conscious of the fact that your thoughts and emotions are connected makes it possible to manage them both. Acknowledging your feelings lets you take control of your thoughts in regards to them.

For example, if you are upset that you get mad at someone you love, you may have some thoughts you don't quite understand. Why would you think mean things about someone you love? Why are you all of a sudden focusing on all of their faults? Well, if you can pause and give space to understand and acknowledge your emotion of anger, you will give light to what is truly happening. Maybe you are feeling misunderstood or not listened to. If that is true, can you think of the event that caused these thoughts and emotions? Now that you remember the event or conversation, you understand why you are angry and what message it is trying to tell you. The communication between you and the person you love didn't happen as you had hoped and now you hide your fear of not being good enough by protecting yourself with mean thoughts and focusing on their faults. It is a simple, primal instinct when you don't feel heard.

If you were in this situation, how do you feel now that you have understood and acknowledged the emotion? Do you feel more in control of your thoughts?

Don't know what to do with emotions. (Most common response)

The best answer I know of is to feel them.

How?

Many ways, but ultimately you need to give them space (to talk) and then a place to go (release).

For example, let's say you are sad after a relationship went sour. Or you are angry after your boss did something completely unfair to you. Talk about it with someone. Allow the emotions to flow. Don't judge them or hold them back. Once you have talked it all out and let the emotions out you will feel better.

Ok to feel

If you have a bad day and don't feel like your normal happy self, that is OK! Your title, identity, or current situation won't be compromised if you admit you are struggling. It is not a sign of weakness.

Accept that you are human. It is ok to feel. It is ok to feel what you are feeling. It is okay to experience emotions (yes, even if you are a guy).

Emotions are real and are part of life. Invalidating them simply makes the person doubt themselves. If I am sad or angry and my parents or friends tell me, "Don't be angry" or "There is no reason to be sad" I begin to doubt my feelings. I ask myself, "Then why do I feel this way? If I am not supposed to, and my friend obviously doesn't feel that way, why do I? There must be something wrong with me."

See how this happens? A well-intentioned friend or family member could cause me to doubt my feelings. When I can't trust my own feelings, I feel I can't trust myself. I then begin to doubt everything about myself. I hate feeling like that and begin to isolate myself. I feel I can't relate with anyone else who feels differently. Because I am alone, I am attacked by negative thoughts and don't know what to do about them. I begin to turn to coping mechanisms. I think the world would be better without me. Thus the cycle begins.

Acknowledging emotions

People who aren't used to considering, discussing, or exploring emotions can find it uncomfortable or even scary. Education, reminders, and practice will help.

Take a moment to close your eyes right now and take three deep breaths. Get rid of any distractions in your mind and pay attention to your body. Pay attention to your lungs expanding as you breathe in. Notice how you feel when you exhale.

What emotion(s) are you feeling right now? Can you name one?

You aren't weak or complaining if you express an emotion (or when you talk to someone about how you are feeling). You are taking care of yourself and connecting at the same time. You don't need to apologize when you bring up your emotions. Just make sure the behavior doesn't poorly affect someone else.

When we are angry that we are angry or upset that we are sad, we are not allowing our emotions to deliver the message they were meant to deliver. Emotions are natural. We can control them, but first we must understand them. Not doing so is like spraining your ankle and getting mad at your ankle for getting sprained. It just doesn't make sense. You need to examine the ankle, understand what it is trying to tell you (you fell, you need to slow down, and you won't be able to run for a few weeks), and then bandage it appropriately. If caught early, you may be able to do this yourself. If time passes or it is a more severe injury, you may need to seek professional help.

Most people avoid acknowledging their emotions either due to not knowing how or because they don't want to face them.

Emotions must be validated. Otherwise, that energy has nowhere to go and will be trapped inside your body until you release it. Then you try to deal with that trapped energy by turning to unhealthy coping mechanisms.

So much of the world's pain and problems can be traced back to the misunderstanding, invalidation, or lack of resolving of emotions.

If parents invalidate the emotions of their children, their children turn to drugs and sex for other feelings.

Invalidating or not acknowledging our emotions can turn into a limiting belief: "My experience isn't nearly as bad as someone else's. Therefore, I shouldn't feel the way I do."

It doesn't matter how dramatic your experience was, the feelings you have are valid. Do not compare yourself to others and their emotions.

Even trying to compare your pain to someone else's is simply you telling your emotions "You don't know what you are talking about." That is denying your own emotions. Instead, do what you have learned in this book and listen to the message you are meant to receive, and then you can let your emotions move on.

If you have been taught that emotional pain is just part of growing up or simply a part of life, then at least you now know that you aren't alone in this. Everyone has had emotional pain of some sort. Rather than suffer alone through life with no hope of relief, why don't we band together and support each other? Why don't we help each other heal and live a full life so we can build our dreams?

Your emotions are valid. No need to deny them.

***

If a child has a difficult problem, his parents should support him in learning to cope with it. If the problem at hand is insignificant (a label only the third party would place on it), then talking about it certainly won't hurt. When your children have a problem they'll come to you because they know you offer more than platitudes and lectures. You really listen.

People who know how to understand and acknowledge their emotions,

> "Do better in terms of academic achievement, health, and peer relationships. They also have fewer behavior problems and are better able to bounce back from distressing experiences .... They'll know how to concentrate, how to get along with peers, and how to handle strong emotions (without turning to coping mechanisms)."
> John M Gottman

Someone I know very well once expressed her reaction to her visit through the Holocaust museum. The experience deeply disturbed her and made her doubt some foundational ideas she had been taught while growing up. As she expressed her feelings and doubts, I could see that those listening were getting nervous that she was saying something like she no longer believed in her faith or that she was considering some self-harming behavior. Even if those thoughts had crossed this girl's mind, that wasn't what she needed at this moment. I could tell she was just trying to be heard and to have her emotions validated. I jumped in, and with the help of one of my sisters who also understands emotions, we helped this girl validate her emotions and release some pent-up anxiety from this memory she was sharing with us.

Trauma that is acknowledged is trauma that can be healed.

When someone expresses their emotions, don't jump to conclusions or expect to have to solve some catastrophe. Just listen and see what needs to be done next. If you listen and ask them what they would like from you, they will often be able to tell you what is needed. The key is to fully listen so they can feel truly heard.

One person may walk through the Holocaust museum and think nothing of it besides it being a very informative experience. Another person may be deeply disturbed by what is memorialized there and could leave that experience with some heavy emotions.

When you experience something hard you need to experience your emotions and talk about them with someone. If you do, you will leave with empathy and compassion instead of self-doubt and fear.

Learning emotions at home

Broken homes (where emotions aren't safe or validated) make it so schools have to make up for emotional teaching.

Barbara Dafoe Whitehead wrote in the Atlantic Monthly and described schools in this way:

> "The great education tragedy of our time is that many American children are failing in school, not because they are intellectually or physically impaired, but because they are emotionally incapacitated .... Teachers find many children emotionally distracted, so upset and preoccupied by the explosive drama of their own family lives that they are unable to concentrate on such mundane matters as multiplication tables."

Many of society's problems stem from divorce, fighting couples, or babies out of wedlock. They all create situations where children are raised in an environment not conducive to proper teaching and relationships.

Older children sometimes disengage from their families and seek emotional support in other places. This is why they start to hang out so much with their friends or spend so much time on hobbies.

Emotional pain also applies to bullying. If there are problems at home, students might try to cope by bullying others. They feel powerful, noticed, and all around better. These are ways of coping or being "rescued" from their pain.

> "With no role models to teach them how to listen empathetically and solve problems cooperatively, the children follow the script their parents have handed them – one that says hostility and defensiveness are appropriate responses to conflict; that aggressive people get what they want."
>
> John M Gottman

Have you ever felt that you just aren't good enough for your parents? If so, you are not alone. The fact that this is so prevalent, explains why there are so many problems at school and in life. People in homes where emotions are not discussed, only experienced and ignored, end up seeking refuge from reality by turning to drugs or trying to find some other sense of belonging.

What happens in a home where you aren't allowed (either explicitly or implied by conversation and reaction) to feel sad, angry, or afraid? You start to think you aren't like your parents at all because your parents don't seem to have all the bad and dangerous feelings that you do. You learn that because you have these feelings and they don't, there must be something wrong with you. You are a problem. Their world would probably be perfect if it weren't for you and your emotions. Now you feel lonely. Now you turn to distractions. You try not to feel at all. You turn to addictive behavior. You turn to violence. You consider suicide.

What is the antidote to an experience like this? Listen to and validate your emotions. Express yourself to a loved one or trusted professional.

Daniel Goleman, a psychologist known for his work on emotional intelligence, said that in a family,

Emotional Pain

> "The greatest mistake physicians make is that they attempt to cure the body without attempting to cure the mind; yet the mind and body are one and should not be treated separately!"
>
> Plato

Did you know that the brain experiences emotional pain the same way it does physical pain?

Recall the story about the elephant with the rope tied around its ankle at the beginning of this book.

If the trainer placed a rope around the adult elephant's ankle, the elephant looked down and thought, "There is something on my ankle. *It hurt when I tried to move*; therefore I will not move."

This happened even though the rope wasn't tied to anything! That is because, to the elephant, the rope represented years of unresolved emotional pain. It felt the pain from years ago as if it were fresh.

5 Reasons why emotional pain is worse than physical pain:

1. Memories trigger emotional pain but not physical pain

2. We use physical pain as a distraction from emotional pain – not vice versa

3. Physical pain garners far more empathy from others than emotional pain

4. Emotional pain echoes in ways that physical pain does not

5. Emotional pain but not physical pain can damage our self-esteem and long-term mental health

Coping with Pain

Just like how we all experience physical pain of some sort, I believe we all experience a type of emotional pain. The problem is that we don't know how to deal with emotional pain as well as we do physical pain.

ACKNOWLEDGING EMOTIONS

"We learn how to feel about ourselves and how others will react to our feelings; how to think about those feelings and what choices we have in reacting; how to read and express hopes and fears."

Don't invalidate a child's feelings. Don't make children distrust their feelings. Otherwise, they will begin to doubt themselves and look for consolation elsewhere.

Listen with understanding and then help them understand their feelings. Your role is a coach, not a judge.

Statements of understanding should precede statements of advice.

The same applies to you.

EMOTIONAL PAIN

Have you ever sprained your ankle? What happens if you don't take care of it properly?

It gets worse.

What do you do to compensate for that sprained ankle?

You limp!

How does that affect the rest of your body?

Your knee hurts, your hip aches, and your back goes out - all because you try to live a normal life without properly addressing the injury and pain.

Have you ever broken an arm? What happens if you don't take care of that properly?

It gets worse.

What would you do to compensate for that broken arm?

Would you say, "I am fine. I am just going to deal with it until it goes away"?

Sounds a bit more ridiculous, right?

If you are injured physically and don't take care of it properly, you try to compensate, or cope, in unhealthy ways.

Now let's talk about emotional pain.

Let's say you have been trying really hard to grow your business. You have been at it for a few years and have tried everything you can think of but it feels like all you have gotten is failure.

What are some emotions you might have in this situation?

Are you happy, peaceful, or excited? Probably not. More likely, you experience one or more of the following emotions. I like to use the acronym BLAST.

Bored

Lonely

Angry

Stressed

Tired

How do you cope with these emotions? Can you relate to any of the following?

Binge-watch your favorite TV show

Eat

Sleep

Video games

Get busy and try to forget about it

Drink

Some form of sex

-

When your brain experiences pain, it wants to numb, hide, or relieve the pain so it tries something to see if it will work. Your current coping mechanisms are your brain's attempt to resolve the pain.

There are neurological reasons why this happens. When the brain experiences pain, it looks to what has helped in the past and it will return to that solution every time.

Let me give you an example.

Imagine a hill with freshly fallen snow. You are the first person to sled down that hill. Because the snow is fresh, you can take whatever route you want down that hill. You can decide your route for maybe the first 2-3 times, but after that, you have created a path in the snow. It would take some significant effort to deviate from that path.

The same logic applies to the brain. After responding to pain the same way a few times, you will have created a path for the brain to follow when it experiences pain. The potential problem here is that if your pain isn't truly resolved, your brain may look to stronger things to find relief. What began as "harmless habits" could escalate to entrenched habits or addictions like drugs, alcohol, and pornography. Your brain may even look to violence or suicide.

These unhealthy ways of coping may be defined as serious problems and those who experience these may be looked down upon. But what many don't see is that these problems are actually symptoms of the true problem: emotional pain.

I want you to pause in your reading and take out something to write with. Write down your answer to this question: "How do I cope with my emotional pain?"

_____

_____

_____

_____

_____

_____

Emotional pain is something that hurt in the past and still causes pain today whether it happened yesterday or years ago. It is the feeling of discomfort (or unpleasant experience) that comes from unresolved emotions.

Think of it like having a splinter stuck in your hand and you haven't removed it. It affects your past memories, your current self-concept, and your confidence in the future.

In short, you know you have emotional pain if you have unresolved emotions and you find that you keep turning to behaviors that don't serve you.

What causes emotional pain?

It isn't the experience that defines your emotional pain. It is the invalidated emotions. It is the emotion you associate with the event. An extreme positive emotion is a positive memory that keeps coming back. An extreme negative emotion is considered trauma.

In other words, how is it that two people can experience something similar (be it "traumatic" or not) and have completely different outcomes? It has nothing to do with the severity of the experience. Arguing this point is just trying to validate your emotions. From a flippant remark to severe abuse, the emotional pain can be the same or drastically different.

For example, how is it that someone can live in a concentration camp and come out so happy? Is it because his experience was less harsh and less traumatic than someone else's? No. It is because he learned and chose to resolve his emotions. Because he validated his emotions, he was able to choose which emotions he kept.

It doesn't deny the fact that he experienced what he did. It doesn't invalidate all the pain and emotions he had. It simply shows that one experience doesn't outweigh another in terms of emotional pain. Ask Henry Flescher.

Henry wasn't known as Henry while at camp. He was known as 177153. That number still remains on his arm. It could be a reminder of his emotional pain – to the point that he can never get over it. But he said it is a "testament to the past. It shows I survived. And I'm here, and loving life!"

He also said, "I never had anxiety or depression." In today's world, that probably sounds preposterous!

How can some survive hellish experiences and others live privileged lives and come apart at the seams?

Probably more well-known is a man by the name of Viktor Frankl. By the time he was 40 years old, he had lived through two World Wars, spent three years in Nazi concentration camps, and lost his parents, wife, and brother in the Holocaust. Yet after all this, he said the following:

> "The mental reactions of the inmates of a concentration camp must seem more to us than the mere expression of certain physical and sociological conditions.... Even though conditions such as lack of sleep, insufficient food, and various mental stresses may suggest that the inmates were bound to react in certain ways, in the final analysis, it becomes clear that the sort of person the prisoner became was the result of an inner decision and not the result of camp influences alone. Fundamentally, therefore, any man can, even under such circumstances, decide what shall become of him-mentally and spiritually. He may retain his human dignity even in a concentration camp."
>
> Viktor Frankl

Viktor demonstrated how Focus, Meaning, and Emotion got him to a place of acceptance - even after what he went through.

Think of a time you were in a group. It can be a meeting or just a group of friends hanging out. You really want to feel like you belong. You want to feel heard. As you try to participate, you feel like no one is listening. In fact, as you try to talk, you notice one of your friends looks at you in a way that makes you think they are bugged that you are even trying.

In the moment, you may experience emotions such as embarrassment, doubt, fear, and even anger. You may be tempted to ignore the group because you tried so hard and you feel you failed. Why try again and have to face those emotions?

Experiment

I want you to try something with me. Imagine this same scenario from the perspective of someone just watching the group from 10 feet away. Pretend you have stepped out of your own body and you are someone else watching you and your group during this scenario. What do you see?

Maybe you see a group of friends spending time together. It looks like people are respecting one another. You notice one person is a little quiet but is trying to participate. You notice that when that person says something one of the friends looks at them and gives them some of their attention.

Now how do you interpret the scenario? How are the two feeling? What do they find important in this interaction?

You see how it isn't necessarily the event that hurts? The same event happens but there can be many different reactions. It could be a basic experience that is no big deal and is even soon forgotten for one person, while for another this could be the reason they have social anxiety.

Sometimes a new perspective can change the entire meaning of a situation.

Relationships and Emotional Pain

Think of an emotion that you have been holding on to for quite some time. Anger, sadness, fear, grief, etc. If you trace it back, you will likely find that it has to do with a relationship of some sort.

A child hears the parent say she will never have a normal life.

Child abandoned by parent.

You break up with "the one."

You were yelled at or fired by your boss.

The customer screamed at you.

You broke your commitment to yourself.

Argument with a loved one.

All of these hurt so bad because you just wanted a healthy connection with the other person and you feel like that connection was severed or even shattered. You don't understand why the event happened and you take it out on yourself. Or you do understand why and you feel it is too late to fix it.

I believe the deepest emotional pain comes when you have hurt or been hurt by somebody. In other words, deep emotional pain comes from a relationship that was hurt. We interpret the unresolved emotions to mean we are different from others and will never be able to connect as we would like. That memory of the relationship affects how we feel about ourselves. Until we address this, we will always think we are not good enough or that something is wrong with us.

The deepest human fears are that you are not good enough and if you aren't good enough you won't be loved.

How connections can heal emotional pain

Although emotional pain can come from hurt relationships, that makes it even more important to have strong connections with people who love you and can help support you.

"People need people." We are designed to connect.

Humans are happiest and most successful when they are listened to, understood, and taken seriously. Sometimes you don't have to solve their problem. You just need to feel with them. Then they feel seen and understood.

Most of us are struggling with something. That doesn't mean we are all broken. It simply means we have something in common and can now support one another.

So much healing can come from connecting to others while experiencing emotional pain. I had the privilege of meeting a man named Chad Hymas. He is a member of the Speakers Hall of Fame and is an incredible man. He lives in a wheelchair because 95% of his body is numb as a result of a massive bale of hay breaking his neck when he was 27. In his story, he shares how he felt completely useless to his wife and kids knowing that he no longer had the normal use of his body. He was planning to fake it for a while and then end his life. But when his wife and kids visited him in the hospital one day and he saw how they didn't judge him one bit and that they loved him anyway, he regained the resolve to live. By connecting to others, he was able to heal from his emotional pain.

It isn't a paralyzed body that makes someone want to commit suicide. It is the shame, embarrassment, and hopelessness that cause the brain to look for a "solution."

I didn't reach out to others until I felt I had no choice. I reached out to my parents for help and then my therapist. As I felt better and better about myself (because I started to understand what I was going through, instead of constantly beating myself up while lost in what I didn't understand), I began to open myself up to others and allow people into my life.

If you have some unresolved emotions that are causing you pain, I hope you don't wait until you have no choice. Please reach out to someone and connect. Put down the book and call or text someone right now. I'll still be here when you get back. I promise.

People just want to be seen and understood for who they really are beneath all the emotions, scars, mistakes, etc. We are all people just trying our best.

Apply what you are learning:

What will you do differently after today?

What are you doing that you should stop?

What are you doing that you should start?

What are you doing that you should continue?

Awesome! Now go share this with someone.

My Story

> *A Heart Like His:* "*Our stories are what make the difference, and if we can tell them honestly we can hope to help each other. In the end, we have nothing to offer each other but our stories.*"

> *I am not ashamed of my story. It makes me who I am today. To be ashamed of it is to be ashamed of who I have become. I know better now than I knew then. Therefore, I do better now. When I open-heartedly offer my story to you, both of us feel less alone. We both feel braver, stronger, and more completely loved.*

Stories are powerful because they give voice to thoughts that make us feel. We relate to those thoughts and feelings. We don't relate as much just by talking about emotions in an academic sense.

When we are vulnerable with our own story, we give others permission to share theirs. When we open up about our emotional challenges, admitting we are not perfect, we give others permission to share their struggles. Together we realize there is hope and we do not have to suffer alone.

If you don't believe me, go read anything Brene Brown has written about vulnerability.

I could tell you a bunch of stories about how to be successful and build your dreams. I could tell you that to love yourself, you need to just be positive and focus on all the good things about you, that you need to surround yourself with people who will lift you up, and you need to remember all the reasons that you are loved. Those are all important. But what I want to do is address what stops a lot of people from loving themselves in the first place - what holds a lot of people back or makes them feel stuck: emotional pain.

If you don't understand and acknowledge your emotional pain, and instead only focus on "positive thinking", when you have your hard days you will begin to doubt yourself even more because you haven't processed your emotions. They will be there, nagging you to acknowledge them while you are focusing on "positive thinking." Eventually, you will start to doubt yourself because this "positive thinking" stuff was supposed to work but it isn't working for you so there must be something wrong with you.

Positive thinking is very powerful. But it is even more powerful when we do what is necessary to address our emotional pain and the limiting beliefs we have about ourselves.

I had tried many of the "goal setting" and "positive" behaviors (church, temple service, activities, etc.) and I still doubted myself. I did all the right things. I attended the motivational seminars and read the self-help books. I would think to myself, "This is all great, but it doesn't apply to me because…" Because I had much that I hadn't resolved for myself. So simply focusing on new behaviors didn't resolve my emotional pain or negative self-talk. It didn't resolve my negative sense of self.

If you turn to certain behaviors to try to hide the pain, your pain will still exist. My goal is to help you heal from your pain so there is room for everything else.

Yes, I know the principles of "where your focus goes, your energy flows" and "focus more on what you want than what you don't want and you are bound to get what you desire." I know those work. But I have learned how important it is to also be honest with yourself and learn to resolve emotions that might be holding you back because they haven't yet delivered their message.

Now on to my story.

If any of you know me, you may be surprised that I even wrote a book that talks about emotional pain and learning to love yourself. Many people have said I have a "picture-perfect" life.

Yes, I am very fortunate to have the kind of life I do. There are so many good things for which I am grateful. I want you to also understand what happened behind the curtain.

I was blessed to be raised in a supportive family that instilled strong values, especially a solid work ethic. Throughout my youth, I was highly engaged in various activities, excelling in both academics and extracurriculars. My achievements continued into college, where I earned a scholarship and excelled in Human Resources.

When I returned from my two-year church mission in Brazil, I was determined to make a career in computer science. Microsoft gave me a fancy new laptop and paid me $10/hour to demonstrate their brand-new products. It was exciting to have access to the latest technology! I was delighted with this job and convinced it was the right path for me. As part of my job, I had to demo the new products to 40 people each week and if I got more, I could earn prizes. After completing my classes for the day, I'd go out looking for people who would allow me a few minutes of their time and then ask them if they wanted to hear about some of the new features of Windows 7.

For a while, it was easy to get people's attention and then, as I kept gathering those easy yes's, things began to get harder. People started saying no and I felt personally rejected. It seemed that they were rejecting me rather than just the demonstration and it caused doubt in my abilities; soon enough, I was only doing the minimum number of demos each week and sometimes even struggling to achieve that.

At first, I enjoyed talking to people but I soon began to notice that it was a lonely job. I longed for some connection. Most of my friends were either in class or at work in the afternoons. So I chalked this job up to something that "wasn't for me" and Googled a few "what should I be when I grow up" quizzes to try to help me know what to do with my life. Have you seen the Jason Bourne movies? You know Pam, the director of the people trying to find Jason? I was supposed to be someone like that. Now I just look like Matt Damon...

The quiz also mentioned lawyers and something about employees. I spoke to a counselor at school and they suggested Human Resources (HR). I knew nothing about HR but decided to take the Intro to HR class.

I absolutely loved it.

HR seemed like common sense to me and I really excelled in my classes. In one class, the teacher graded on a curve system; when it came time for the final exam, all the other students pleaded with the professor to not include my test score because they didn't want me skewing their grades.

I was much more confident about myself again!

I ended up receiving the Outstanding Graduate award in Business Admin and HR and went on to complete my Masters in HR.

My career in HR skyrocketed, I was hired as an intern and my boss really believed in me. Then that boss left and I took her position. I was excited to be able to grow so quickly - swiftly rising to lead the department, and contributing to the company's impressive international expansion. I earned respect and trust from colleagues worldwide. After a few years, I was seen as an executive in my 20's. I had a new car, a nice house, and was traveling the world. I was a leader in church, talented in sports, and had a great life.

Why do I mention all this about me? Can you see the picture I am trying to paint here?

I told you a lot of the good things in my life, not to brag, but to establish two mindsets or labels that became associated with me.

1. I had a "picture-perfect" life.

2. I was used to success and I was used to getting it on my own.

These two things are important to understand because they explain why my emotional pain hurt so badly and affected me so much. Later you will see that I used them as coping mechanisms.

Now let me share with you some experiences that contributed to my feelings of emotional pain.

All my life I had a plan ahead of me: Finish high school, serve a two-year religious mission, finish college, get a job, buy a house, get married, etc. When I returned from Brazil, that plan started to fall apart.

Dating

Upon returning home, I knew that the next steps were to finish college, get a good job, and get married. I went back to college the day after I got home. I got a job as soon as I could. I dated a lot. I knew marriage was important and I enjoyed being with girls. I had set goals on when to have a first date, when to have a girlfriend, and when to get engaged. I was going to meet all those goals (even the last) and I was so excited! I had learned about the power of goal setting on the mission and I was about to see it work outside of the mission! But in the end, I decided to call off the relationship. The girl I was dating (and with whom I thought we were pretty serious) had been dating someone before him leaving on his two-year mission and was "waiting" for him to come home so they could get married and she was still confused.

Because of this, I felt I had been burned. I did everything I was supposed to. I set goals, found a good girl, treated her well, and progressed towards marriage, only to find out that this whole time she was waiting for someone else! I was furious. After that, I started to disbelieve in goals in regards to dating. I now had some new beliefs: "If someone is waiting for a missionary, stay far away." and "Don't get your hopes up with dating because it probably won't work out anyway." I had done everything I was supposed to and it didn't work out.

I am not saying I got everything right the first time, but you have to remember that I was used to being successful. Normally, I would create a plan, follow it through, and I would come out on top. If I didn't, I would be able to talk to my professor or someone in charge and we could figure out what else I could do. But my "success" with dating (marriage) wasn't coming like I thought it would.

I was disappointed and confused. For the first time, I had real feelings of "now what?"

I continued to date, but the relationships either ended because of a lack of mutual interest or because I felt that God wanted me to end it. This happened often enough that it became really upsetting. I finally met someone really special and we started to like each other and then I felt I had to break up with them? It just didn't make sense - I was trying to find someone to marry, follow God's word and do the right thing, but each time I got close to "success", I'd have to end it. Eventually, I again started to numb my emotions since they kept getting crushed.

After years of trying for so long with no success, it became hard to try with dating. Why try when I "know I won't be successful"? I even said to myself, "Why can I be successful in everything but dating?"

I did well in school, work, sports, and music. Those gave me results for trying. But it didn't seem to work that way with dating.

My thoughts of "now what" had turned to "so what?"

I began to be disenfranchised. (Being disenfranchised can make you feel like you don't belong or that you have no power). I stopped believing I could get married. I turned apathetic. It was easier to just not care.

(This book is not just about dating. If you are thinking, "Oh no! Just another rant from a single guy" I hope you stick around. I included this in my story for two reasons: 1. Everyone dates and can therefore relate in some way. 2. This is part of my story and I am not ashamed of it. I have come a long way and learned valuable lessons about loving myself even when I felt I lacked what I wanted most.

I don't need you to feel bad for me. But I do want you to feel with me.) (Sympathy vs empathy)

As I started to get older (yes, I thought 22 and 23 was old) and my friends began getting married, it became increasingly difficult to be joyful for them. Instead, I felt as if their successes highlighted my failings - I was left feeling unhappy and lacking self-confidence due to comparing myself with others. I was experiencing a new kind of failure and I didn't know what to do about it. By the time I had reached 22 and 23, this feeling of inadequacy was starting to take over.

"I am successful in everything I do! People respect me for my accomplishments and for who I am. Why can't I be successful at this?"

Because of some "failed" attempts and lack of success, I began to doubt a lot of things.

I went through a time of dating just to date and only going on one date with each girl. I hated the roller coaster of getting my hopes up with a girl, having my feelings all of a sudden turn off, getting disappointed, and having to recover. I began to believe that it was better to just protect myself by closing myself off. I was tired of the disappointment and being vulnerable just to have it not work out. Even then, I continued to date because I had to show I was putting effort in when people asked me why I wasn't married yet.

I hope you can see how limiting beliefs and emotional pain were starting to build up here. <u>They were reinforced by the story I was telling myself.</u>

At the time, I had no idea what was happening to me. All I knew was that all my friends were getting married (leaving me) and I had to protect myself more and more from my failure. Because I had unresolved emotions (emotional pain), I had to put up shields to protect me from more pain.

WORK

At first, I was excited to report to my new boss because he was one of the top executives and had promised me so much support at the beginning. I was happy because everything seemed to be going in the right direction.

Then one day, my boss told me, "We have nothing against you, Ben, we just hate HR."

Can you imagine what I felt when he told me that?

I was passionate about Human Resources and what it could do for the business. But when they said they hated HR, it felt like they were hating me too. I felt like people saw HR (and me) as a necessary evil rather than a valuable asset. I felt like HR wasn't appreciated or valued enough, no matter how hard I tried to explain its importance and help out. Despite all of my hard work, I felt like I wasn't quite good enough.

When I was in school, church, or anywhere else outside of work, people always seemed to value my ideas and look to me for solutions. I felt respected and necessary outside of the office, but now working with people all day long, that same feeling didn't return.

I began to wonder which set of opinions was true. Was I finally being told the truth because I was in the "real world" now? Were people just being nice in school and at church? I felt confident and respected outside of work. Inside of work I felt undervalued, unappreciated, disliked, and simply tolerated. What feelings were right?

Have you ever felt this way at work? Not sure you are in the right place? Not good enough?

Work and dating were all linked to the feeling of "These are important parts of my life and they aren't working. Something must be wrong with me."

My experiences with dating and work led me to doubt my own feelings. I was inexperienced with my feelings and fled from them. That caused me to isolate myself from others – and then it became harder to develop deep relationships. I felt I knew a lot of people, but only superficially. I was president of the choir, played sports as often as possible, spent a lot of time with friends, was head of an HR department, was a leader in my church, and spent every Saturday morning serving others. On the outside, to everyone else, it looked like my life was perfect and I was and should be very happy. I may have even appeared happy.

But deep down I was suffering in silence. I felt like an empty shell. I felt distanced from others. I felt I only met with failure with the things that were important to me. Sure I had a lot of good things going in my life, but not everything I wanted. Everyone in my life said I was amazing in everything, but when I went to work, I felt like my boss and coworkers - the people who should support me the most - doubted my abilities and even looked down on what I did. Don't they see that I know what I am doing and that it can help them?

Can you relate to anything I have said so far? Life seems good and you have done everything you were supposed to, doing all the right things, but you still feel stuck and unfulfilled?

Let me add another part of my story and why it has to do with emotional pain.

Because I had unresolved emotions, I began to be vulnerable to behavior that goes against my values. In other words, since I didn't know how to resolve my emotions, whenever I felt bored, lonely, angry, stressed, or tired, I would look for ways to "check out" or "cope" with my emotions. What may have begun as reading or watching TV, moved on to wasting time on YouTube and other social media. That certainly turned off the mind and I would find myself hours later still watching that "one" video.

After a while, these behaviors just didn't do it for me and I entered the world of addiction to try to cope with my unresolved emotions. The addictive behavior was so appealing to my brain because it seemed to "fix" the feelings I didn't want. It gave me counterfeit feelings of love, connection, and excitement.

Because my brain learned that this behavior "worked" I would continually turn to it if I didn't like how I felt. But my brain ended up needing more and more of it. After participating in that behavior, I would feel bad because I knew it went against my values. It left me feeling empty, guilty, and disappointed in myself. After a while, I began to hate how I felt and I hated that I kept turning to the behavior. Of course, I couldn't tell anyone, especially my parents, because I was taught to know better than that and to not participate in that behavior. I began to hate myself. I hated how I kept giving in. I felt I was living a double life. I was drowning in shame. I couldn't tell anyone because I felt like I had to live up to their image of me.

Why, even after serving people, would I turn to that behavior?? I could understand why I would need the "emotional fix" after a stressful situation or being lonely, but why after a good thing like service?

My brain began to see my addictive behavior as not only a stress reliever but also as a reward or as a sign that I could finally relax.

Here's where addictive behavior can start to affect other parts of your life. Because your brain associates an "emotional fix" with the behavior, it learns to rely on that behavior to feel better.

Have you ever wondered why you don't want to hang out with your friends or family when it doesn't make sense to feel that way? Maybe you have said to yourself, "Why do I feel so closed off when I visit the family? It is like I don't want to go sometimes. It is like it is very transactional and I don't want to open up."

If I went to a family event and began to focus on all the things I didn't have and how I didn't relate to any of them, I would begin to have a conversation with myself. "This is dumb. I am not having any fun. They are all talking about things that I don't have and will probably never have." These thoughts caused me to feel lonely, stressed, and maybe angry. I then, subconsciously, would start to associate these unpleasant feelings with hanging out with friends or being with the family.

My brain knew that it could feel better if I left the party and participated in the addictive behavior.

This explains why, even during family events (where you would think family love and closeness would help the situation), someone may end up participating in addictive behaviors. It is because of the triggered, unresolved emotions and negative self-talk.

This went on for many years. I wasn't happy at work, I was dating just to check a box, and I was turning to this addictive behavior as my only emotional solace.

Eventually, I hit a point where things had to change.

As I considered the possibility of a real relationship with a particular girl, I was hit by a wave of panic. I had finally made it past the first date with someone and we had been spending a lot of time together, but I felt my addictive behaviors still lingering in the back of my mind. How could I be honest with someone, let alone this girl I was with, if I couldn't even be honest with myself? I wanted to keep things going with her, but at what cost? If I stayed like this and didn't take action, wasn't I just going to hurt her in the end?

I had finally allowed myself to believe that I could have something real with this girl. Our connection was growing and I thought maybe, just maybe, this one would work out. But suddenly, a dark fog of realization descended as I comprehended the magnitude of my addiction. It had pervaded my consciousness, shaping how I saw her and how I saw others - tainting my vision of reality. At that moment I knew things could not continue as they were; I had no choice but to seek help and rebuild myself from the ground up.

I finally called my parents and desperately uttered, "I need help."

Thankfully, they listened and were willing to help me.

I broke things off with the girl and joined a recovery group. There I realized I wasn't the only one struggling. I saw that other people - who looked like amazing people on the outside - also struggled on the inside. This gave me an incredibly huge desire to change and to help others.

These people became so confident in themselves. They knew they weren't bad people. They knew they weren't beyond help. They knew what they were doing was simply a choice their brain had learned to see as a solution. A choice they now realized they had power over. Even when they tripped up and made a mistake, they still knew they weren't bad people.

They teamed up with God. God now became an ally instead of a careless bystander.

Solutions that were always there and had been within my grasp now became possibilities.

Rather than turning to God, I turned to coping mechanisms. I didn't turn to God because I felt He wasn't answering my prayer in regards to marriage and therefore I felt prayer wasn't working for me. Of course, now I know that He was helping me the entire time and was preparing me for something better than I could have imagined.

You see, when we get a splinter in our hand, we can be told about Neosporin and bandages. We can be told that the wound will heal and you just need to move on. We can even place a bandage over it, but none of those things will work if you haven't removed the splinter.

In the world of emotions, I believe it is more common than not for people to misunderstand how they work. Emotions are personal and most have found them to be uncomfortable. Therefore, when this type of person is presented with a situation where someone else is dealing with emotions, they don't know what to do. It is easier to ignore it or replace it with distractions or simply "anything else."

Speaking from experience, the metaphorical bandages being offered to me didn't work because I still had a splinter in my hand. Even the Master Healer couldn't heal me because I had closed off and wouldn't let Him look at it.

My experience kept me stuck in the Behavior section of the model. My emotions were numb and my thoughts were so negative I thought I was broken. When our emotions are numb we strive to feel something. We still have emotional needs. But our list of emotions is much smaller. Generally, we feel angry all the time (a protective emotion) and seek "hits" of pleasure to make us feel better. This is when we turn to unhealthy coping mechanisms.

Emotions exist and we need to realize that a person who is struggling with an addictive behavior or even someone who appears to have a perfect life on the outside, may be facing a terrible battle inside. The toughest part is that they are trying to fight that battle alone. It is exhausting because they are fighting themselves. They don't understand where the voices in their head are coming from. Therefore, the person believes them and enters this spiral of shame and self-loathing. They don't want to tell anyone for fear of being judged so they stay in silence and have to do things in secrecy. They are convinced that they are the problem, that they are not good enough, and that there is no hope for them.

Do you know anyone like this?

I wanted so badly to rid myself of this addictive behavior and resolve my emotions, that I reached out to a therapist. I overcame the thoughts of, "Wait, I am already investing in this recovery group. I am tight with my spending and now I will have to pay even more for a therapist? Do I really want to do this? Maybe I can just figure it out on my own." I wanted to make sure I took out the splinter completely. I wanted nothing left – no tiny excuses to remain and give me a chance to return to old habits.

In my recovery group, I had been learning a lot about emotions and emotional pain and I wondered what my emotional pain was. I then remembered something that happened as a child that I had been running from for years...

***

As I share this part of my story, pay attention to how you think and feel. These realizations will be important in your path to overcoming your own emotional pain.

As you read my story, don't compare and think, "That was no big deal" or "Oh my! That is so much worse than mine!" Rather, see how we can relate. Our experiences may not be the same, but we may relate to how we have felt during our experiences. We are all dealing with something and maybe we can learn from one another.

My story comes from when I was 9 years old. I was in elementary school and we had just finished playing a ruthless game of dodgeball for PE. My friends were starting to realize that I was a natural at the game and I started to thoroughly care what they thought of me.

As we made our way out of the gym (I can still picture it today), we were climbing up the ramp back to class, and my friends were laughing hysterically about something.

Naturally, I wanted to be a part of the fun so I asked them what was so funny.

They told me to raise my arms.

I slowly complied - only to notice with horror that my armpits were drenched in sweat. My friends laughed even louder at this unfortunate discovery, as though it was something repulsive and undesirable. Utterly embarrassed and suddenly extremely conscious of my body, it felt as if every onlooker knew what had happened.

It felt like the world was crumbling beneath my feet. All I wanted was to fit in with my peers, and here they were mocking something completely out of my control. What could have been mistaken as a normal part of any energetic athlete was now magnified and deemed disgusting by those around me. This led me to believe that there must be something very wrong with me; something so grotesque that others would recoil in disgust at the sight of it.

Embarrassment crept its way through my veins until fear took over. Here I was, a 9-year-old boy, stuck in an embarrassing situation with emotions I did not yet understand. Humiliation, shame, trepidation, and discomfort filled the air around me like suffocating smoke from an angry fire.

At that moment I believed I was disgusting, unwanted, and unworthy - feelings that quickly morphed into self-loathing and shame. I couldn't talk to anyone about it, so I simply kept silent, storing away these painful feelings for some other day.

This event marked me that day; leaving an indelible scar in my mind that would take 20 years to heal.

"Ok, fair enough. But is it really such a big deal? Wasn't it a one-time event? Isn't it just a rope around your ankle?"

It turns out I have what is called, "hyperhidrosis," or excessive underarm sweat. Because I didn't know how to control it, I learned to go through life trying to hide this part of me. I would go to group activities like game nights or dances. I would try to be involved and have a good time, but I hated it when we would do something where I couldn't hide my sweaty armpits. Whenever someone discovered it, they would react like they were grossed out. It brought back all the painful memories of that event in elementary school. Each time it happened, it made me want to hide it even more because my feelings of embarrassment and shame got stronger and stronger. I still couldn't tell anyone about it.

So I did my best to be successful in a lot of things so that people could see me and instead think, "Wow, he is so great!" I wanted people to think highly of me instead of seeing me as disgusting.

Years later, a close friend of mine told me that I keep people at arm's length. It was true. I put up a shield of success because I didn't want people to get close enough to possibly discover a part of me that I have no control over and I am not proud of. Why would they want to still hang out with me if they knew this part about me? I do not want to go through that pain again. I don't want them to find out that I am gross or that I am disgusting...

***

I had tried to hide this part of me for 20 years, never telling anyone because I didn't believe I could share it without fear or judgment. When I finally mustered up the courage to confess all to my therapist, I could feel the trepidation rise up in my chest as I spoke. I was sure he would think me disgusting and wrong, but after I finished speaking, he just looked at me with kindness in his eyes.

My mind raced with confusion; why wasn't he judging me? Wasn't that what everyone else would do if they heard this deep secret of mine? Was he treating me like a normal person despite knowing the truth?

My therapist then did something extremely helpful. He helped me reprogram my brain and rewrite my memories. You see, emotional pain lasts so long because the brain connects memories to emotions and pain. If we experience something traumatic, the brain tries to hide it or numb it because it hasn't been able to relieve it. If we trigger anything related to that experience, all the memories and emotions can flood open and overwhelm us.

The only way to overcome that is to do what therapists call "reassociation." The brain has learned that $x = y$. If x happens, y will happen. If I go to a game night and someone discovers my hyperhidrosis (X), they will laugh or be disgusted and I will be embarrassed (Y). Nobody would want to be with me. Why? Because it happened in the past and my brain has "proof." Do you see how quickly that happens? We then try to cope with all those emotions in our old ways. We have to change the equation so that $x \neq y$ in all cases.

My therapist helped me reprogram my mind by telling me to close my eyes and imagine I went back and met my 9-year-old self right after this event by the gym had occurred. I would take him to a safe place. I would tell him, "You just experienced something really hard and you have every right to feel the way you do. But I want you to know that it is over. You are loved. And you are going to accomplish some amazing things in your life."

As soon as my therapist suggested that, I scoffed. How could these words be true when everything around me seemed so hopeless? I can't lie to myself! It isn't over and why in the world would anyone love me?

Tears streamed down my face, and as I repeated the words from my therapist a few more times, I finally let my emotions come out. The fear, the embarrassment, the shame I had been suppressing for so long began to melt away.

Because I finally processed my pent-up emotions, I was able to reprogram my brain and see things in a new light.

That experience is no longer traumatic for me.

I have learned to turn that memory from a ghost that haunted me into an ancestor that I can learn from.

Speaking to another person in a safe setting, someone who could really comprehend my struggles and aid me through them, was incredibly empowering. With any addictive behavior or struggle, I can't emphasize enough how important it is to get it out of your mind. Suppression leads to depression. The opposite of depression is expression. You need to talk about it with someone.

In my experience, I realized I didn't feel loved. I felt this way because of some experiences I had and I repeatedly told myself stories that destroyed my sense of self. I felt like a failure. I felt unlovable.

What I wanted most was to feel loved - that is why I chose all of my behaviors and coping mechanisms. As it turned out, the new behaviors didn't resolve it for me. To let love in, I had to let my emotions out. In order to receive love I had to learn to see myself as worth loving.

God is my Support

As I overcame my emotional pain, things changed. My therapist helped me see things differently. God helped me see myself differently. I saw that I was turning to my addictive behavior, not because I was a bad person, but because I was attempting to understand and meet my emotional needs. I stopped seeing myself as the enemy. I knew that Satan was the true enemy and was putting destructive thoughts in my head and causing me to doubt myself. I saw myself as worthy of God's love and began to allow Him back into my life. He healed me from the inside out and I am so much better because of it.

Ezra Taft Benson said,

> "The Lord works from the inside out. The world works from the outside in. The world would take people out of the slums. Christ takes the slums out of the people, and then they take themselves out of the slums. ... Christ changes men, who then change their environment. The world would shape human behavior, but Christ can change human nature" ("Born of God," Ensign, Nov. 1985, 6).

As you learn to see yourself differently - with a higher perspective (ideally a spiritual perspective) everything will change. This is what is meant by the quote,

> "True doctrine, understood, changes attitudes and behavior. The study of the doctrines of the gospel will improve behavior quicker than the study of behavior." (Elder Boyd K. Packer (Oct 1986 General Conference))

God's doctrine teaches an eternal truth and you choose to mold yourself to it. The doctrine that you are a child of God, when understood, helps you see yourself differently, believe differently about yourself, have different thoughts, feel differently, act differently, and get different results.

Your willingness to accept truth determines your ability to move forward with life.

Satan distorts truth and makes you see yourself as less than you truly are. When you can see things as they truly are - naming your emotions, knowing they don't define you, seeing Satan as the true enemy, and strengthening your knowledge of how God sees you - you change from the inside out.

***

Why do "good people" struggle with addictive behavior?

The answer is because of unresolved emotions (emotional pain), negative self-talk, and a wounded sense of self.

"Good people" often find that they "can't" admit they are struggling with something. They feel like it goes against their reputation. People would look differently at them.

Leaders "can't" admit they don't know everything or that they are scared.

Entrepreneurs "can't" admit they are worried about how to grow their company.

Parents "can't" admit they get angry at themselves or that their family isn't "perfect."

Men "can't" admit they are lonely and just want love and connection.

Women "can't" admit that they aren't happy with who they are.

I was successful in pretty much everything I was involved in and therefore "couldn't" ask for help or admit to someone that life wasn't as amazing as it seemed. Even then, sometimes, because of lack of training, if I were to reach out to someone and say I was struggling with loneliness, addictive behavior, or lack of self-love, that person may react judgmentally. They may say, "It is just part of life and you have to get over it." Or they may not understand and be overwhelmed – thus affecting the relationship. None of these reactions are helpful. "Getting over it" hadn't worked thus far...

By validating my emlotions with "You have every right to feel the way you do" I resolved my emotions and changed my behavior, I entered a state where I mastered my thoughts and communed with infinite intelligence. This is my quest now. I have achieved and become much more than I ever thought I could have.

***

You now see that over the years I was having a lot of emotional pain building up: rejection, embarrassment, feelings of not being good enough, confusion, fear, shame, etc. The more I realized it in me, the more I began to see it in the eyes of others.

This is when I learned about a missing link. Companies can spend millions of dollars on motivation and goal setting, but if emotional pain still exists, then the employee will hear the motivational material and say, "Yes, but that doesn't apply to me because..."

Now, please don't misunderstand me. I am not saying everyone has some childhood trauma that prevents them from getting work done. I am saying that some people have amazing potential but are held back by a wounded or limited sense of self. If they were given the tools to overcome that, their potential would be unleashed.

I hope you are either relating to what I am saying or now beginning to understand the problem that exists in the world today. People too often focus on and judge behavior and leave emotions out of it, when emotions and self-talk are at the heart of everything. We relate with our emotions. Understanding and acknowledging our emotions (and those of others) brings connection and empathy. Instead of walls of judgment, we create bridges of understanding.

Apply what you are learning:

All change starts with a decision.

What are you learning about yourself?
What emotions are you feeling?
What do you want to do about it?

Awesome! Now go share this with someone.

Processing emotions

Gaining power over your emotions

> *Three things happen when we experience an emotion. First, our body generates an emotional vibration. Second, we begin to feel the emotion and any thoughts or physical sensations that come along with it. Third,* **we choose to let the emotion go** *and we move on, after a few seconds to several minutes. This last step is called processing, and once it is completed, we have successfully moved on from the emotional experience and it shouldn't cause us any problems.*
>
> The Emotion Code

While speaking at a conference, a girl in the audience raised her hand and asked me a question. I will call this girl Kandice. Kandice wasn't rude or disrespectful, but I could tell she was coming from a place where she didn't quite believe what I was talking about. I told her I would talk to her after the meeting to more fully answer her question.

I met with Kandice after and discovered she was extremely angry at the world. She was one of those people that you thought were just waiting to jump down your throat and cause a problem. She would ask questions in a way that made you think she was just waiting to say something like, "That doesn't apply to me." Or "that can't work." She had given up on the world and was just plain angry.

In my professions, I have learned the importance of listening. When Kandice asked her first question, I knew there was more to it. So I asked her to share more. Rather than jump in and lecture her with all my knowledge, I listened to her so I could understand the core of what she was going through.

She said my speech really touched her and she decided to ask me some questions. She began to open up and tell me a few things about her life. I listened in a non-judgmental way and got to know her a bit. She shared a few examples of what she was very angry at or just didn't believe. I could tell that she had become a little apathetic towards some things and was rebelling towards life. But mostly, she was angry. She was angry about how her mother-in-law had treated her for years before she died. She never felt good enough. I saw that underneath all the anger she was hurting and scared. She loved her family and just wanted her new family to have a good life.

After fully listening, I felt inspired to encourage her to write a letter to her deceased mother-in-law. In this letter, she could express all her pain, anger, and worry. And then she could burn the letter. She agreed to do so.

I stayed in touch with Kandice and reconnected a few weeks later. She said that after she wrote the letter, she was able to let go of her hate. She no longer cried every time she thought of her. Later, I helped her realize that she could take a few minutes for herself each day and simply write down how she was feeling. She was pushing so hard for what she wanted that she wasn't able to take care of herself.

Unresolved emotions don't just give up. They find a way to manifest themselves – even in ways that you wouldn't like (like with a loved one; during an important, yet stressful meeting; or while taking a test).

I stayed in contact with Kandice for a few more months. The difference in her attitude and outlook was evident. She was no longer that angry girl. She was so much happier. She was more open with people and was making important connections. Her relationship with her own mother and husband improved and she had the courage to start her own business.

When you're filled with stress and suppressed emotions, it is like a balloon so full it is ready to burst. You must be very careful when around this balloon, making sure nothing touches it or it will pop - so you isolate it from other things. Does this happen to us as well? When you are full of suppressed emotions, do you feel more connected to others? Or do you isolate and have to be very closed off around others?

Many of us have been conditioned to suppress our emotions. For some, it's because of early life experiences, such as having to "suck it up" or feeling unsafe to express oneself. Maybe someone told them not to cry or something traumatic happened and they weren't able to process their emotions. Others learn from watching others around them; that when people express their emotions, people get hurt; someone gets crazy angry and blows up on someone. Someone cries uncontrollably and it is awkward or the person is seen as a baby. Some learn that expressing emotion is seen as unpleasant or immature.

Maybe you never learned how to process. Maybe you never had a safe space to do so.

Despite this conditioning, feelings will inevitably surface. The key is catching them while they're small and manageable, rather than after they've grown into messier, overwhelming forms. Even when emotions are huge and messy, there is a way for you to release them and move on. It may take time and it may take professional support, but you can gradually express the rage, anger, pain, fear, sadness, grief, shame, etc. Doing so allows a much-needed release from the pressure of carrying them for so long.

Give yourself permission to feel what you are feeling. Don't judge your feelings off the book of "how you are supposed to feel."

Feel to heal.

"I give myself permission to feel and that doesn't mean I am weak or a failure."

Once you learn to understand and acknowledge your emotional pain, you gain power over it. In order to understand and acknowledge your pain, you need to remove it from your brain.

Imagine you have a splinter in your hand. How do you heal from that? You take it out!

As a child, how did you remove a splinter if you were unable to do it yourself?

You took it to a parent.

Why? What did they do?

They removed it, cleaned and bandaged the wound, and, most importantly, reassured you that everything would be okay. That special feeling of safety and reassurance from a loving guardian helps to alleviate pain and encourages healing processes so that you feel secure as a person.

It is fascinating how we learn such vital lessons in our childhood but tend to forget them as adults. We think we can cope on our own and try to ignore the pain until it gets worse and then don't know how to communicate our issue so we find unhealthy ways to manage it. It's similar to looking at your hand expecting your blood cells to disintegrate a splinter - it doesn't work! The same principle applies mentally; if you don't remove the pain from within yourself but instead try to think it away, it won't help.

Even in dating, it is important to process your emotions as early as possible. Otherwise, people look for "rebound" dates and may even fall into temptation because they are looking for "happiness." If you don't learn to manage the emotion of anxiety, you will look for "liquid courage" or some other drug of choice to mask the emotion.

Depression after dating or ending an engagement is real!

So how do you get an emotional splinter out of the mind? You can *talk* about it or you can *write* about it. These make up part of your power (PWR) over your emotions.

PWR

P - Pray.

Talking about it gets the splinter out of your mind. The best person to talk to is the Master Healer (God) through prayer. You could also talk to a trusted friend, parent, coach, or therapist.

I had to change the way I prayed. Instead of just saying things like, "I went to work today. I had a test and broke up with Sally." I told God my emotions. "Today was tough. I broke up with Sally, my test sucked, and I heard my boss say some things that I didn't like and it has really affected how I feel about myself. I am sad, frustrated, upset, and lonely. I don't like to feel this way but I am feeling this way and I need to feel it today."

Dale Carnegie said,

> "Ever since the days of Freud, analysts have known that a patient could find relief from his inner anxieties if he could talk, just talk.

> Why is this so? Maybe because by talking, we gain a little better insight into our troubles, get a better perspective.... All of us know that 'spitting it out' or 'getting it off our chests' brings almost instant relief."

We all get scared sometimes. The natural thing is to hide your fear and not let anyone know. But that makes you stagnant. When you admit your fear to a trusted person you will find that you are not alone and you have incredible people around you who are ready and happy to support you in your dreams.

Why is it so important to talk about it? So you can make room in your mind to believe the words telling you that you are great. You have to be willing to be healed and believe it can be done. Believe you are worth healing.

Talking about it is the first step to change.

I got the emotions out of my head so I could understand, acknowledge, and finally do something about them. Guess what? Many times, all that is required of you is to let the emotions out of your mind. Once the splinter is out, your hand can do the natural thing and heal itself.

Your body is designed to heal. Did you know that?

Talk it out. Don't just grumble and moan about it. Find the strength to tell someone you trust how you're really feeling. Doing so with the intent to understand and acknowledge your emotions, will allow you to find solutions to your current situation. Of this I am sure.

W - Write

If you are not comfortable with the first step because you aren't used to praying to God in that way or you just aren't ready to tell anyone about your emotional pain, write about it. But don't write in your journal the same way you always have. Write out your emotions. Even better, if part of your emotional pain involves another person, you can practice overcoming that emotional pain by writing a letter to that person. Whether you send it is a different thing. Once you get all the emotions out of your head you can decide what to do with the letter. You can burn it or tear it up or rewrite it. I'm telling you, once you get it out of your mind, all sorts of possibilities open up. If it doesn't work the first time, keep trying. You will know when you have gotten all your emotions out.

I have included a few writing prompts to help you get started:

"Dear (God, mom/dad, future/past self, etc.),

I am having a hard time today. I feel very _____ (name your emotions).

Today I want to overcome my emotional pain from _____ (write how you feel about that memory).

> I don't know where to start, but here's how I feel about my life right now (name your emotions)."

So many people feel lost because they feel they have been betrayed by believing in a dream that never came true. A hope was crushed. Often, it is related to love or something they treasure.

Take the movie "I Can Only Imagine" (based on a true story) as an example. The main character, Bart, had dreams of his own, just like any other child. His father had dreamed of playing football as a child but that aspiration was crushed due to an injury. He had spent many years trying to drown that sorrow in alcohol and made sure that his boy knew that dreaming about something was a waste of time.

Because his father was so angry and frustrated all the time, his mother ended up leaving. Desperate to impress his dad, Bart joined the football team, though it was never his true passion. He broke his leg at some point and had to quit, which upset his father even more.

Bart eventually found solace in music only to meet more disappointment from his father who thought such pursuits were foolish. This led to Bart's decision to move out.

After months of performing on the road, Bart was still frustrated because he just couldn't get his break with his music. His manager listened to his frustrations and learned about his relationship with his dad. He then said,

"Stop running from it. Write about it. Let that pain become your inspiration.... Then you will have something people can believe in."

That is when Bart wrote the song, "I Can Only Imagine." It became a huge hit.

Instead of fleeing from your emotions, you can use them as a source of creativity and motivation. Start writing about them and feel the pain transform into something beautiful.

R – Reach Out

The brain seeks a way to relieve pain, so it reverts to what it is familiar with. Now that you've realized and discontinued your old coping mechanisms, there's an emptiness left in its place. Even after reading this, you may still feel the urge to do what you used to do as a means of handling your emotions. The solution lies in replacing that void with something new. If you're tempted by old patterns, reach out to someone for help, or try serving someone else.

This meaningful connection has been my main source of strength while working through my emotions. When you make a meaningful connection, it creates positive chemicals in your brain that displace the desire for negative coping habits.

When life looks bleak and hopeless, turn towards people. They can fill up all those holes. It's easier to cope when you have a support system—just knowing that you don't have to struggle alone often makes things less burdensome.

Think of something tough that you have gone through. Now think of how you are dealing with it. How many of you are still running from it? Trying to hide from it? Staying so busy that you can't think about it?

Guess what? Because you are hiding from that, you can't be found by the good. Because you are running, you are passing by good things.

You have to experience the emotions you are running from so you can rewrite that memory. Turn that ghost into an ancestor. Then you can stop only existing and start living.

If you find yourself in this situation, find someone to help you.

Write down three people you can reach out to right now. You can either send them a message about what's going on in your life or simply check in and ask how their day is going. Either way, sometimes reaching out to someone else can be just as helpful for them as it is for you.

Stay connected, my friend.

1.

2.

3.

What thoughts do you have on these PWR principles? How would this help you?

We all have "moments of clarity." What do you do during those moments? Do you write down what comes to mind? Or do you let the moment pass you by?

Emotional Stacking

Allowing your emotions to stack is like having a pressure cooker. At first, the pressure is low but the longer you allow it to build up, the more explosive the result will be.

Why is it that one day you all of a sudden blow up at your spouse because they left the dishes in the sink again? It isn't like the fact that there are dishes in the sink is going to ruin your life. It is because over time, you allowed something you focused on to start as a small annoyance, grow into frustration, then anger, and by the time you get to the fifth occurrence where they left the dishes in the sink, you are ENRAGED!!

This is emotional stacking.

One occurrence of dishes left in the sink wouldn't cause you to blow up at your spouse. But if you don't address the emotions while they are at their low levels, they have no choice but to build up pressure.

As you go through life, you will have experiences of all kinds. Since you, as a human being, assign meaning to everything, you assign meaning to those experiences and therefore begin having thoughts about what has happened and is happening to you. Those thoughts influence the emotions you have.

Many people don't understand this. They don't understand that we control our emotions. Most think emotions control us and are therefore scary and should be avoided at all costs. Anger, fear, and sadness are looked down upon. They think anger is explosive and sadness is depressing; that emotions either lead to catastrophe or should be medicated as soon as possible.

The trick is to express your emotions constructively.

Catch the emotion while it is at low-level intensity and you don't have to act out to get attention.

Releasing emotional tension

Emotions are energy in motion (e-motion). Positive energies turn counterclockwise. This is why we feel so good and expanded. Negative energies turn clockwise (contraction) – that is why we feel tight. Negative energies dissipate when we talk about the emotions, label them, and feel understood. It is like you are unwinding that tension. Let your e-motions out.

Know how you feel. Own how you feel. Then you can change it.

We have a thought, then a feeling, and then we create stories that explain why we feel that way. For instance, something may happen that gets us worked up, and we feel negatively toward another person in response. We justify our feelings by creating stories to explain why the feeling is there in the first place. This cycle continues until our emotions are processed.

Here is an example of how my wife and I were able to process emotions and unwind some tension.

While writing this book, my wife and I were renovating our kitchen. As the weeks went on, it began to take its toll on us. Fatigue and stress were weighing heavily on us, coupled with a sense of frustration at living in the constant mess. During one particularly stressful night, we stayed up late to finish mudding and sanding patchwork. My father-in-law and my dad had both stayed late to help out, but now it was just my wife and I trying to tie up loose ends before we could finally call it a night. My wife cleaned the area and moved tools to another room while I worked on something in the kitchen. As I searched for the tool I needed, she told me with irritation that it was in the other room. Taken aback by her tone, I registered thoughts of resentment in my mind - why did she expect me to know where it was when she was constantly moving things around without telling me?

Since it was a small comment and I wasn't sure why she said it like that, I could have let it go saying it wasn't a big deal. In fact, in the past, I definitely would have just moved on because I didn't want to get angry or show my frustration about this because I didn't want it to escalate and turn into an argument. But I remembered that I needed to bring things up while they were small, so I asked my wife a little later why she was so upset that I didn't know where the tool was. She told me she had spent the last 40 minutes cleaning and moving tools and she thought I had watched her move things. I had not.

Once we got our small emotions of frustration out and cleared the air with mutual understanding, we were able to move on.

That event is no longer something that is suppressed and adds pressure to a teapot. This is the importance of expressing (processing) emotions and not suppressing them.

Prisoner to your emotion

You become a prisoner of your emotions when you are a victim of the past. Our prisons (coping mechanisms) are different but they are all attempts to feel better. If you are not a victim of the past, you won't engage in behavior to simply feel better. You will do things you enjoy as you look to the future.

Acknowledge the pain and grieve any loss you have experienced. Then forgive those involved (including yourself). **This is how you overcome emotional pain.**

Healing yourself helps heal others.

> "It is not my fault that my life has been screwed up to this point. But it is my fault if my life is screwed up after this point."

You can change and rewrite your story at any time.

Find what works for you and then give yourself permission to do that.

As you learn to understand and acknowledge your emotions, you may run into a moment when your emotions are harder to process. Check in with yourself – if the emotions persist, you might want to reach out for professional help.

Speaking from experience, I don't like going to the doctor. I try to avoid it as long as I can. But when the pain is so great or I am worried I will hurt myself even more, I finally go to the doctor for help.

Can you relate to how you treat your emotions? Sometimes it is hard to see and realize how much you are hurting because of unresolved emotions. Maybe you don't want to go to the doctor because it isn't bad enough, you think you can handle it on your own, or maybe you just don't want to be judged for how you are feeling.

Seeking help doesn't mean you are broken. Rather, it means you realize you are dealing with something that maybe you aren't meant to fix alone.

Whatever the source of your emotions, validate them and then ask yourself, "Do I want to remain hostage to these emotions or do I want to release them and gain my freedom back?" Once you make that choice, miracles can happen.

Imagine what you could do once you were free of a trapped emotion!

What is your outlet?

An outlet is different from a coping mechanism. An outlet is what you do to express your emotions in a healthy way. A coping mechanism is something you do to feel better instead of expressing your emotions.

Many people go to the gym or run marathons as their outlet.

Entrepreneurship can be amazing, rewarding, and so worth it. It can also be lonely, stressful, and discouraging at times. It is important for entrepreneurs to have an outlet.

One of my clients is a successful entrepreneur who has made millions and is very capable in business. He went through a divorce 14 years ago and when he told me about his ex-wife it was all about how she never believed in him, never supported him, and it was never worth the conversation.

I asked if his relationship with his ex-wife had been strained right from the start. The answer was no, but over time they both became guarded with their feelings because of poor communication which eventually resulted in them drifting apart emotionally.

In contrast, his current wife brought tremendous joy to their relationship. If they ever argued, he wanted to work through it quickly so they could go back to having fun together. He knew his new wife trusted him and valued his opinion. He knew she believed in him and cared about what he had to say. He often talked to his new wife about things and had a frequent outlet with her. Because they talked through things often and early, their relationship has stayed healthy.

When emotions are expressed, they don't affect your sense of identity. His unexpressed and unresolved emotions with his ex-wife turned into unhealthy thoughts about her and himself. He no longer believed in himself because he felt stuck, hurt, and offended. He now knows he is worth better things and is happily creating a better life for himself. He is able to move on and assign better meaning to things that happened in the past.

Expressing emotions while they are small is simply a good practice for a healthy relationship.

Men need help knowing it is okay to acknowledge and work through feelings. They will come off as more compassionate. They will connect better with their wife and loved ones.

> "For most men, becoming emotionally aware is not a matter of picking up new skills; it is a matter of granting themselves permission to experience what's already there."
>
> John M Gottman

If you have a habit of expressing emotions through healthy outlets, you will more easily master your thoughts and thus be in a position to see yourself as capable and others as regular humans instead of idiots.

NNFF technique

A powerful technique to help you process your emotions is the NNFF technique.

(N)Notice it. Notice your emotion and where you feel it.

(N)Name it. Name what you feel. Naming puts boundaries on the emotion and gives you control over them.

(F)Find it. Find the opposite emotion that you want instead.

(F)Flip it. Flip what you are feeling to that new emotion.

This technique gives you clarity and direction. It helps you recover from the undesired emotion and helps you focus on a desired emotion.

To help you transition to a new emotion, you need to let go of the energy associated with your current emotional state and do something that you can link to the new emotion. You can do this by doing something productive or enjoyable that helps you express or release this energy - like writing, creating art, exercising, talking, etc.

Stories we tell ourselves

"Change your story, change your life"

Are your stories empowering or disempowering? Do you tell yourself stories of how it can be done or how it can't?

Remember the elephant story? Although the emotional pain was valid, the story the elephant was telling itself was disempowering. It kept saying, "There is something on my ankle, it hurt when I tried to move, therefore I will not move." If it can change its story, it can change its life. This comes with a change of perspective.

If you can see the world differently, the world you see becomes different.

What story do you tell yourself each day? That you just aren't good enough? That you will never get anywhere? That you will always have the problems you currently have? Or that you can do this? That you are creating something amazing that will benefit so many people?

Maybe you are choosing to hold on to your emotional pain. Maybe you are so used to having the pain that you don't know what life would be without it and are therefore afraid of making the change.

The stories you tell yourself can completely define or redefine your life.

When I went to therapy, my therapist asked me to name five positive memories in the past ten years. I seriously struggled to think of more than one. Why? How had that happened when I had a lot of amazing things happen in my life? It happened because I had conditioned myself through my internal stories to only remember the negative and delete the positive experiences from my memory.

I traveled to New York and Spain on two separate occasions with two different choirs. You would think those would be great memories. However, I had gotten so good at telling myself stories that my life sucked and there wasn't anything good going on, that I would reclassify these experiences as bad memories. Even if 95% of the trip was great, I would focus on the 5% that was bad and color the entire experience that way.

When I was captain of my high school swim team, I was tasked with anchoring the 4-man 400 Freestyle relay. Though I raced with all my might and gave it my best effort, we lost by a mere .4 seconds. That is faster than it takes to blink! To make matters worse, a picture of me and the other guy finishing that race was on the front page of the sports section in the school paper the next day.

Here I was, the captain of the swim team, and I had lost that race because maybe I didn't stretch my arm out enough.

I could have chosen to let that experience devastate me. Sure, it was embarrassing and my coach definitely talked to me about it, but I could have let it really bring me down and doubt my ability to be captain.

On a more long-term basis, I could have let this experience define my entire swimming career. I could have said to myself, "After 4 years of swimming and being entrusted to lead a team, you make a tiny mistake that costs your team the race. Your whole swimming career was a failure."

Imagine what kind of emotions would come if I told myself that story!

Besides my coach, I don't know if anyone else ever brought up that event to me. In other words, it wasn't as big of a deal as I could have played it out to be. Everyone makes mistakes. Mistakes don't need to color your entire life.

The stories we tell ourselves define how we experience life.

You are the author of your life. You can change your story.

You can transform:

Challenge into Exploration

Uncertainty into a Sense of Adventure

Fear into Resolve

Risk into Reward

Addiction to Recovery

Weakness to Strength

If you are thinking, "This is just another 'fake it until you make it' idea," I want you to consider something with me. You may think changing your story is just being "fake." You may even consider it being "untrue" to yourself. Let me put it another way to see if it will help you change your perspective. I invite you to "<u>face</u> it until you make it."

As you saw from my personal story with hyperhidrosis, faking it didn't work. Just trying to change my story did feel fake. But when I finally faced the pain and the memories, I was able to rewrite the story and change my ghosts into ancestors.

You can do the same as you learn to face what you are going through so you can change your story.

Remember the benefits you will get from changing your story. If you are experiencing stressful and inhibiting emotions now because of your current story, imagine how free you will feel when you change your story to one that is more empowering!

Feelings of anxiety come from incorrect beliefs about ourselves. "I am irresponsible." "I can't do anything right." "I will never be able to figure this out." These beliefs cause panic attacks.

Change your story!

"I am capable." "I do big things for God." "This is going to work!"

All you need is certainty. You can have certainty about something that hasn't happened yet. You create your own certainty.

If your story is limiting (a "limiting belief") you are blocking your own progress. Limiting beliefs are like being isolated at home and forgetting that there is a sky, mountains, and other people outside your house. The good news is that you can challenge and overcome your limiting beliefs!

Too often we allow negative self-talk (negative stories) to destroy our self-image. How do you talk to yourself while brushing your teeth?

Change your story!

Be proud of your story – including the imperfect parts. Take responsibility for it and use it to do good in the world. Tell yourself the right story and you will get there.

You are the author of your story. Make it an empowering one! Make your "mess" your message. Have confidence in your story and you will become an inspiration to others.

Ask better questions

If you don't know how to understand your emotions, you will have the correct mindset and work on a new behavior but will experience an emotion like fear or anger. Fear and anger misunderstood can derail your behavior and destroy your result. Not knowing this, you will start to doubt your thoughts and beliefs. "I did everything I was supposed to. I even changed my story. What is wrong with me?"

Wendy Watson Nelson once said,

> "If you want to change your life, change your questions."

Don't ask "What is wrong with me?" Ask, "What happened to me?" The prior question will take you down a spiral of discouraged thoughts. The latter question will allow you to analyze an event and then understand and acknowledge what you got out of it. Then you can decide what to do with it going forward.

There was a girl who was part of the deaf community. She was told she wouldn't graduate high school because she couldn't hear. She was told she would be another bad statistic. At first, she would ask herself, "Why can't I hear?" Later, she changed her question to, "How can I hear?" She ended up getting cochlear implants so she can hear and now has a master's degree, and her own business.

Ask and ye shall receive. Ask better questions and you will receive better results.

Change "What if I am the only one struggling with this?" to "Who can I talk to?" "Who can help?"

"How else can I see this?" "How would I like to see this?"

The Tapestry of Emotions

In the realm of hearts, we find our base,
Emotions, the essence of the human race.
Yet oft we battle, try to hide or flee,
From feelings that affect both you and me.
A common thread, we all can share,
Yet voicing them, we often fear.
On screens, a sea of smiles so bright,
Yet darkness dwells within our night.
"I'm not alone in feeling low,
Though social streams a different show.
Sadness grips, and fear takes hold,
Is it alright? Am I too bold?"
A tough day comes, a heavy heart,
It's fine, you're still playing your part.
Your value stands, it won't depart,
Strength lies within, it's a work of art.
In highs, in lows, and all between,
It's what makes us sharp and keen.
To feel, to stumble, then to rise,
To see the world through wiser eyes.
Through trials faced and tears let flow,
You'll find the strength in you to grow.
Life's tapestry, with colors rife,
Is woven through its joy and strife.
Reach out, connect, let love be drawn,
From those who've been through dusk to dawn.
On sturdy shoulders, let them lend,
Their strength, their love, to be your friend.
In every laugh, in every tear,
In every shadow drawing near,
You're human, brave and full of grace,
Emotions woven in every trace.

Summary of Chapter 8

- Learning the language of emotion is like learning a new language. It requires belief in one's ability, patience, expanding emotional vocabulary, and consistent practice.

- Emotions serve as messengers from our inner selves and play a crucial role in connecting with others. Ignoring emotions can lead to a sense of detachment.

- Understanding and acknowledging emotions empowers individuals to control their emotional responses, ultimately leading to healthier relationships and improved mental well-being.

Questions for Application:

- How can you apply the concept of "emotional stacking" in your own life to prevent emotions from reaching explosive levels?

- Reflect on a recent situation where you experienced a strong emotion. How might acknowledging and processing that emotion have led to a different outcome?

- Consider an area of your life where a lack of self-confidence is holding you back. How can you challenge negative thoughts and build genuine confidence in that area?

Chapter 9 - Behavior: How Do You Manage Your Behavior?

Addictions. Habits.

Actions.

What should I do?

Sometimes we don't consciously choose our feelings. But we can always choose our behavior.

Any change in how we understand the brain ultimately affects how we understand human nature.

Let's say you really want to lose 20 pounds. You have tried going to the gym but it just hasn't worked. You get on social media one day and you find a new diet that "really works!" There are tons of pictures of others who have tried it and lost even more than 20 pounds. It makes sense so it is worth a try. You start following the new diet but it is confusing and you have to do it every day. You miss some of your favorite foods and you went on vacation last week and didn't follow any of the diet anyway. A few weeks later you just aren't seeing any results so you give up on the diet.

Fast forward a few months and you still want to lose 20 pounds (now possibly 25...). You really want to find the best solution for you. You would love the "magic pill" that just makes the pounds fall off. You have talked to friends, scrolled social media, read articles, and listened to the news. Your head is full of ideas on how to lose those pounds.

You know what you should do and yet you find yourself procrastinating and you just don't do it. Why?

Because you have been focusing only on the behavior and results. You haven't gone deeper to address what goes on inside your head. You haven't managed your identity, beliefs, your thoughts, or your emotions. You have not linked those to the new results that you want in a powerful way that engages your beliefs and your emotions. You haven't visualized it in a powerful way.

If you want to lose weight you might say, "I want to lose 20 pounds." Then you might think, "I need to try something different (new behavior) so I need to exercise every day until I lose the weight (result)."

So you start exercising. But when you have to set aside an hour a day to do it, showering afterwards, dealing with sweaty clothes, or needing to buy equipment or go to the gym - well, it can be discouraging. Because the process is only as deep as behavior you quickly think "This is not working. I'm going to do something else." You keep trying different things but nothing works so your brain stops believing that you ever will get any results from your efforts. This reinforces the belief that nothing you try is going to work, so why bother? You are doomed to be overweight. There must be something wrong with you because you can't lose weight. Your identity changes as well- "I can't do hard things. I can't set goals because they won't happen anyway because it's too hard and I'm not capable. People will never love me because I'm overweight."

Do you resonate with any of this? Do you know anyone who has gone through a process like this?

Now that you understand what is happening, you can reverse the process to make it work. How? Follow me here.

You decide to lose weight. Why? What is your sense of identity right now and how will this be affected? You think, "I need to lose 20 pounds." Why? "Because I think it will make me feel better." Why? "Well, I realize that I am overweight." Okay, what does that mean? What does that mean to you and your sense of identity? Are you happy with how you look and how you feel? Because it is not the number that is the issue but how you feel about the number that is the issue. It is the story you tell yourself and how you see yourself that is the issue. Are you following?

Can you see yourself 20 lbs lighter? What does that look like? What does that feel like? How does that person act every day?

The proper way to make a change with your body is to powerfully link to what you want and not focus on what you don't want. Most people would say, "I don't want to eat as many donuts. I don't want to weigh this much."

The more powerful thing to do is to say, "I want to feel amazing. I want to feel energetic." Thinking that way will eventually have you saying, "I love my body. I have the energy I need to accomplish whatever I want. I am energetic and so happy!"

Talking like this is talking about your sense of identity. The story you tell yourself is empowering, encouraging, and motivating. When you talk like that you feel like you can do anything and because you feel like you can do anything your natural behavior is to do something towards getting the result that you want. You know that to get more energy, you just have to move your body. It can be any type of movement. You move for the sake of moving and that gives you more energy. And guess what? As you start to move more often and more energetically you start to burn calories! You start to care more about what you eat. It's no longer motivated by guilt but it is motivated by your positive sense of identity. You know how amazing you are, you know how much you are worth it, and you know that you want to treat yourself right. So you make the necessary changes. You begin to surround yourself with people who motivate you. People who see themselves positively, have accomplished what you want, and can help you accomplish what you want. So you join the groups, the gyms, the networking, you hire a coach, or you hire a trainer because your identity is activated and is involved. Because of this you make different choices and treat your body the right way.

If you simply focus on behavior change to get you different results you will become frustrated when that doesn't work and doubt your ability to influence your own behavior in the future.

Try, fail. Try harder, fail. Doubt your ability to change... It is a vicious cycle. This reinforces your destructive thoughts that there is something wrong with you.

This happens because your internal, or subconscious programming hasn't changed. You have created habits and they won't change unless you reprogram them.

If you can understand that all behavior is based on an emotional need then you can start to understand your emotional needs and your behavior will change. Emotional needs are normal. Everybody has them.

Understand your emotions and ask, "Why do I do this behavior? What emotional need is causing this behavior? Oh! Maybe I am bored, lonely, angry, stressed, or tired. If that's the case, what does that mean if I'm stressed? What am I stressed about? Yeah, work was stressful, family was stressful. I tried to do this and it didn't work. Okay, good to know."

This is called reflection and meditation. This is becoming aware. The more self-aware you are the more control you have over this entire process. Because your thoughts begin to change, the stories you tell yourself begin to change.

"I am not the problem. I am not dumb, incapable, or broken. I am simply feeling stressed and I have not known how to satisfy this emotional need until now. My brain thought that this behavior was the only option because this option has worked up to now. Because I can understand that this is all based on the emotional need of not feeling stressed, bored, or lonely I can change the story. I can flip it around and say 'Oh I understand that I'm lonely. What would I like instead?' I'm changing my thoughts based on my sense of identity. The opposite of loneliness is I want to feel connected. I want to feel loved. How do I do that? I reach out to others. Great! As I do so I begin to feel connected. This all works because I took time to observe how I was going through the model and I reprogrammed the pattern. I made a change in my behavior to get the same emotional reward because I understood my emotional need."

See how different this is?

Speakers and books like this are so powerful because they talk to you at this level. They influence your thoughts. When done correctly, this influences your self-concept. If I can influence the way you talk to yourself and the thoughts you have inside your head, I can help you see that you are not broken, that you can do this, that you are amazing, that you have incredible potential, and that you can have a powerful impact on this world and others around you. Imagine the things that you would do with this new perspective and belief. Imagine how you would feel! Imagine how you would treat yourself and others. Imagine how your behavior would change! Imagine what results you would get!

The things you already know, the habits you have, the morning routines that you've been trying to establish, the different ways of eating, the calls that you need to make - all those things will start to happen (behaviors) and will lead you to the results that you want because you have changed your sense of self and you start to tell yourself different stories.

Change your story, change your life. Remember who you truly are and you remember that you can do anything.

If I can lift your sights, you will see more possibilities. Negative self-talk, not processing emotions, or getting stuck on problems brings your sights down. You end up looking down on others, down on yourself, and eventually focusing only on yourself. Lifting your sights helps you see beyond yourself, see others in a better light, and see above the forest you are currently in. Your perspective changes.

***

This all relates to the principles of State, Story, and Strategy. Getting yourself into a positive emotional state has the power to alter the story you tell yourself, allowing for empowering stories to guide your actions. You'll suddenly have access to strategies, either pre-existing or newly discovered, that will help you reach your desired goals. This is why in books like this and when I speak around the world I always start with State and Story.

This explains why it is said that success is 80% psychology/mindset (state and story) and 20% strategy. If strategy was the only answer then whoever found the perfect strategy would have a monopoly. If strategy was the only answer then we would spend our time finding the perfect strategy and we'd only have to implement that. But how many strategies do you already know of to get the result that you want? How many people have given you advice on achieving this goal? Do you already know what you should do? It is likely that you already have at least a few ideas of what you could do to accomplish the result that you want.

Think of what you want right now. Take a few moments and write down three ideas that you have on how you get there...

See?

It isn't a lack of strategy.

Sure you can improve the strategy. There may be a better strategy out there. But if you know the strategy, why don't you do it? It comes down to your self-concept, beliefs, thoughts, and emotions. If you can believe in yourself and tell yourself stories that this is possible, put yourself in the state of feeling this momentum and feeling powerful then you will implement the strategy and get the results that you want.

Michael Phelps is the most highly decorated Olympic swimmer in history. Did he have a different strategy than anyone else? Could anyone else train just as long or just as hard as him? Yes. Would they get the same results? Not necessarily. His coach had him develop a routine before every race.

He listened to music (state). What stories do you think he told himself? He imagined himself swimming the perfect race. He felt each stroke, each turn, each breath, etc. The story he told in his head was one of victory! Yes, he knew the strategy. He had practiced it over and over! But no strategy will get you the results that you want if your state and story are not there.

For example, in the 2008 Beijing Olympics, Phelps was the fan favorite for the butterfly race. Unfortunately, very early into the race, his goggles filled up with water and he swam the rest of the race blind. Here is what he had to say about it.

> "So you know, when I go into 2008 and in the 200 fly, my goggles fill up with water the first 25. And I am blind for a 175 meters. I revert back to what I did in training and counted my strokes. And I knew how many strokes I take the first, second, third, and fourth 50 of all of my best 200 flies. So I reverted back to that and I was ready for that because I was mentally prepared for it."

This shows why strategy alone will not get you there. He prepared his state. He knew his empowering story. And then his strategy came through.

Addictive Behavior

"Maybe I have changed, but I think it's for the better.' I don't need to drown my brain in alcohol every night to prove I fit some artificial definition of cool.... I'm serious about my life."

These principles apply to addictive behaviors as well. It is literally how the brain works on a neuroscientific level. The brain wants something because of an emotional need based on stories that you've been telling yourself that have affected your sense of identity.

There are many ways to describe what you do when you experience emotional pain: self-medicate, cope, rescue, distract, escape, etc. Really it is anything that gives you a sense of emotional relief so you can "feel better". For the purpose of this book, I will use the term "cope." Regardless of the term, you afre trying to solve the "problem" of your emotions by doing something on your own. That could be watching TV, eating, shopping, gambling, or working so hard and so long you have no time to think about them. What starts as harmless distractions can escalate to more mind-numbing behaviors like drugs, alcohol, and sex/pornography/masturbation. They might even lead to violence and suicide.

The things on this list are powerful because they give your brain a temporary "fix." They either numb or replace your feelings.

How many times have you come home from a long day and just wanted to watch TV? Of course, I am not saying TV is bad, but it is often used as a way to distract from the emotions of the day.

Pause and ask yourself these questions:

In what ways am I using busyness, work, television, or the computer to avoid facing something?

In what areas am I so desperately longing for an outcome that it's preventing me from enjoying the journey?

Think of the scenario. Insert your coping mechanism or "behavior of choice."

People use coping mechanisms because they are forms of instant gratification. They feel they lack something and they think these mechanisms can provide it for them—usually a sense of happiness.

We only pursue that which we believe we don't have.

People want connection and to feel fulfilled and loved. If they don't get it from good sources, they will turn to alternate sources.

Anyone who has experienced addictive behavior can relate when I say this. We don't want to be judged by our behavior. We wish we could change our behavior. We need help emotionally.

The dictionary tells us that an "addiction is compulsive engagement in rewarding stimuli despite adverse consequences." In other words, you choose a particular behavior because of how it makes you feel (rewarding stimuli). If there are adverse consequences, people say it is an addiction. If not, people don't see it as a problem.

I am going to avoid the term "addiction" because often people say someone "has an addiction." That connotes the person "has a problem" or they are now defined by something. This quickly becomes a label. I am sure you have heard terms such as "drug addict", "porn addict", or something else. In this book, I will use "addictive behavior." This is because behavior is something we choose based on the results we think we get. The behavior becomes addictive the more and more the brain thinks it is solving a problem. In this case, when it thinks it is feeling relief from emotional pain.

When someone struggling with addictive behavior is called an addict, what they hear is "I don't see you as a human being anymore. I only see you for your filthy behavior."

Do you really think they are going to be able to change if they hear that from others?

Think of it this way. You are not your addictions. You are not your addictive behavior.

Addictive behavior isn't limited to drugs, alcohol, or pornography. It can apply to eating, shopping, video games, social media, etc. You don't hear people calling others "shopping addicts" or "social media addicts." Yet, the psychological reasons why people turn to these behaviors can be the same.

If you struggle with any of the above-mentioned behaviors, I hope you find hope in this book. If you know someone who struggles with any of these behaviors, I hope this book helps you learn compassion.

Recall that the definition mentioned earlier includes the word "compulsive." That explains why many people believe "addictions" are like diseases that have no cure and are accompanied by societal judgment. The dictionary defines "compulsive" as "an irresistible urge, especially one that is against one's conscious wishes." The latter part is why the actor of the behavior feels so bad after the action and why society judges them so harshly. The word "irresistible" often removes the idea of accountability and empowerment from the scenario.

The temptation to act on addictive behavior can feel irresistible. It is definitely intense and includes a lot of brain chemicals. If your craving is strong enough you will ignore all logical reasoning (Emperor's New Clothes example). But our bodies are designed to heal and can always regain the strength to overcome that "irresistible" urge through understanding the principles taught in this book and applying what you learn.

Cameron Staley, a licensed psychologist at Idaho State University, said,

> "[Compulsive behavior] is often triggered by feelings such as stress, anxiety, loneliness, or boredom. To avoid processing these emotions, individuals will resort to a variety of coping mechanisms including eating, going online, shopping, gaming, or viewing pornography.

> If we're not aware of what's going on, we stay in that compulsive pattern and keep viewing over and over again. There are lots of things we can do to satisfy emotions instead of trying to distance ourselves from them."

He continues,

> "Considering pornography as a symptom, and then identifying what's generating that symptom, can help individuals move forward. Whether that looks like identifying an underlying mental health concern, engaging in therapy, receiving social support, better nutrition, increased physical activity, or mindfulness, there are more options than one might think.

> If you notice the urge to view porn, take 60 seconds. And sometimes that's sufficient to notice, 'Oh, there's an urge, what's preceding the urge...' And in a minute, that urge to view porn is gone. It's not like... sit down, meditate, get

your cushion out, it's like slow down for a minute. And allow your agency to come back online."

The coping mechanisms aren't the problem. They are "solving" the problem! When you see the coping mechanisms, ask yourself what the actual problem is that you are trying to solve.

In Maya Szalavitz's book "Unbroken Brain" we learn that fighting the war on drugs is fighting the wrong war. Drugs are seen as solutions for those who suffer from emotional pain. The real war should be against what causes the need for drugs.

She even tells us that alcoholics are running from feelings.

The father in the film, "I Can Only Imagine" had been an aspiring football player, whose dreams were cut short after a serious injury as a young man. He spent the remainder of his life struggling with the emotional pain that came with it – turning to alcohol as a form of self-medication. He slowly lost everything: his wife, home, and nearly his son, until he reached a point where he could no longer endure the turmoil any longer. It wasn't until he finally reached out to God and felt his emotional pain wash away that he changed, gave up alcohol, and got his son back.

Maybe serious problems could be avoided if people felt they could talk about their struggles. I believe this is why people turn to addictive behavior in the first place - they feel they can't tell anyone how they are feeling.

Talk to a trusted friend about it. Supporting each other can bring such strength that can't come in any other way.

The reason this is so vital to understand is because when we strive so hard to do what is right, to reach out for help, or to run from that bad habit, but haven't resolved what is causing the problem, it only becomes all the more exhausting when our "solution" doesn't work. This explains why the addictive behavior has to become "stronger" and more "extreme" to satisfy the person.

We have to uncover the splinter and get help to heal it. Then the unhealthy behaviors that follow those thoughts and feelings will take care of themselves. They will no longer offer anything enticing because there is no longer a hunger to be satisfied.

Discover that you are not the problem and there is nothing wrong with you. Let the emotional wound heal. Connect with others and be blessed.

The Unbroken Brain teaches that the same tendencies that cause one to be very successful can also cause one to be susceptible to addictive behavior.

Cameron Staley shares more about how this works.

> "Often, Latter-day Saints who struggle with pornography are those who have really high standards for themselves, or who tend to externalize their faith a little bit more and are trying to follow their standards perfectly. This creates something of a paradox—if that individual has an unclean thought or looks at a sexual image, he or she feels shame more severely because they did something inconsistent with their values—and the cycle continues."

Proper self-regulation is the solution to addictions - even if it is a person who is considered prone to addiction because of their learning.

Continuously thinking about or reliving a bad memory is like picking a scab. Avoiding it or covering it up doesn't help either. You have to let it heal properly.

When the urge to itch the scab arrives, you have to have practiced a plan on how to not scratch. Otherwise, it will be too easy to give in.

Learning these things doesn't take away your responsibility, rather, it increases your response-ability to properly self-regulate.

Many things can help, but at the base of the addictive urge is an unresolved emotion that the brain is trying to cope with.

All people who have struggled with addictive behavior can relate. We begin by being stressed, curious, or bored and having the initial feeling of "finally I feel happy or free." The more we train our brain that this is how we find relief, the more our brain will start to override our programming and seek out that relief. But eventually, this behavior turns into self-loathing. We hate what we have to do to get the feeling of relief again. We hate how people look at us when they find out we are addicted to that behavior. We hate how much we want to change but can't seem to do so. Nobody would understand and nobody is willing to help. The addictive behavior is the easy solution.

Are you driven by "feeling" better or by "being" better?

"Feeling" better leads to addictive behavior.

"Being" better leads to transformational change.

Do you engage in any self-loathing behavior?

Habits of behavior

People love it when they don't have to make a decision. That is why automatic things like subscription memberships work so well. The brain loves simplicity and loves it when it only has to make a decision once.

In the book "Power of Habit," we learn that the brain works by habits. It creates habits so it doesn't have to work as hard and can create space to devote to something else like learning something new or doing something enjoyable. If the habitual behavior leads to a pleasant outcome, the loop strengthens. If it doesn't, you don't like it and you look for something new. Habits can only be changed if they are understood, reprogrammed, and replaced.

We develop habits with our mindset as well. We have a default mode, or a mode we have habitually entered because of past behavior. It is something you do so often with your mindset that it becomes a habit. Just like how to brush your teeth - you don't have to think about how to do it.

Your brain is continuously being programmed. You are assigning meaning at all times: looking for threats or pleasures. The trick is to set up programs you want instead of allowing outside influences to program you.

Focus on the positive, new behavior you want instead of the negative, old behavior you don't want.

People who say, 'I won't give in today" probably will because now they have feelings of anxiety and stress. The solution is to focus on what you want instead. And believe that it is possible with a correct understanding of addictions.

The power to change is already in you. Believe in you.

We will never move beyond what we have already visualized ourselves accomplishing. Your vision determines where you will get in life.

Associating emotions with actions

All behavior is based on an emotional need. You choose your behavior to either avoid pain or to gain pleasure.

If a child wants to feel seen and loved, but they aren't getting any attention from their parents, they will begin to misbehave or act out until they start to get attention. They will then interpret that to mean that the only way to get attention is to act out.

This realization is key and it all comes down to your associations. In other words, what emotion you associate with an action. For example, if you associate (or link) pain and discomfort (fear, anxiety, or other emotions you don't want to feel) to networking, selling, doing emails, or doing spreadsheets, then you will find ways to avoid doing those things because you don't want to feel the "painful" emotions. You will do easier, more enjoyable things and say you are "being busy." You are busy but you aren't doing the crucial things in your business.

On the other hand, if you associate (or link) pleasure (excitement, enjoyment, etc) to networking, selling, doing emails, or doing spreadsheets, you will find ways to do them more often and you won't mind when you find them on your to-do list.

Notice that the behaviors are the same. But your reaction towards them is completely different based on the emotion you have associated with them.

All behavior is based on the emotions you have associated with them. You avoid or pursue the behavior based on the pleasure or pain you have linked to them.

To go deeper, if the pleasure of eating Doritos is stronger than the pain of being overweight, you will choose to stay home from the gym and snack. But if you see eating Doritos as adding to the pain you feel when you look in the mirror and see your love handles and growing chins, then you will see working out as contributing to the pleasure of having energy each day and being able to feel good in your clothes.

Everything comes down to how you associate your emotions. Once this is understood, you can reprogram your emotional habits.

> "If we find ourselves addressing the same problematic behaviors over and over, we may need to dig deeper to the thinking and feeling driving those behaviors." – Brene Brown

We often focus way too much on behavior when that is just the symptom, not the cause of what is going on.

A client of mine is going through a divorce. Understandably, that is a very emotionally raw experience. He had been nine months sober but decided to go back to drinking because he didn't want to face the stress of the divorce. His brain weighed the options and decided to turn to drinking to avoid the stress of the divorce.

In my coaching sessions, we could spend time focusing on what to do with the divorce or we could focus on the drinking. But until he learns to ground himself with his thoughts and emotions, he will not be ready to make decisions on either of those! In fact, until he sees himself and the situation differently, he will be stuck in his thoughts and won't resolve his emotions so he will stay with his harmful behavior.

It is the same idea when it comes to kids. If they are hungry, tired, and upset because their sibling was mean to them and they had a fight, it does little good to spend time trying to lecture them or asking what they should do next time. They are simply not in an emotional state to do so. After you allow them time and space to process and release some emotion, then you can have a rational, solution-based conversation. This has happened many times with my boys and they often come to me later and apologize for their behavior and say they were tired. In other words, they are perfectly capable of solving the problem if you are willing to help them through their emotions.

My client's mind may be working overtime to try to imagine life after the divorce and what to do now, but he won't be in a place to make those decisions until he is able to process and release some of his emotions.

In other words, there are times when it is appropriate to focus on and improve behavior. But it is most effective when you have resolved and addressed the thoughts and emotions beforehand.

This applies to putting a bandaid on a wound. The behavior is to put a bandaid over the wound and the result is that you feel better. But if that is all you did, the wound would never get better because you never cleaned and treated it!

My client discovered that he was in a drama triangle and kept playing the role of "rescuer" when his wife was going through something hard. As soon as he could give this identity a name (once he discovered he was playing the "rescuer") he decided he didn't want that identity and he changed his focus to what he wanted to become and what his new life would look like after the divorce. This has given him clarity on how to move forward in this stressful time.

Focusing on behaviors brings judgment. Focusing on emotions brings understanding, empathy, and connection.

Emotions and behaviors

Every behavior is based on an emotional need. If you can understand that, you can still meet that emotional need but do a different behavior - one that doesn't make you feel guilt or shame but makes you feel joy. This joy reinforces your belief in yourself. It helps you see and feel progress as opposed to shame which makes you isolate and hate yourself.

This information is the same that is taught in the books "Atomic Habits" and "Power of Habit." They call it cue, craving, response, and reward (I labeled these in the Emperor's New Clothes story). Something happens, you have an emotional need, your brain chooses something it thinks will meet that emotional need, and you have your reward. If you don't notice the pattern, you will think something is wrong with you and that you are helpless to change it. Once you notice the pattern you can reprogram it.

As you do so, you remember and fortify who you truly are. You gain a new identity or sense of self. That new self doesn't behave the way it used to. It is no longer "I can't" or "I won't" but "I don't." "I can't" puts the blame on someone or something else. Implying if you could you would - not taking responsibility for your decision. "I won't" implies you have thought about it and decided in that circumstance it isn't something you will do. "I don't" is a statement of character. There is no debate; no decision to consider because it has already been made. It is simply not something you do.

Including God in this reminds you that you are loved and worth loving. This knowledge helps you to keep trying. It helps you know that you aren't broken and that you aren't the problem - there is nothing wrong with you. You are simply learning how to deal with your emotions and now that you know better you can do better.

It is amazing how well Alcoholics Anonymous works even though it isn't founded in science and many scientists discredit the methods because they can't explain them. Things from God work, even if man can't explain them.

Even if you can't figure out what emotional need you have, the fact that you are thinking about it puts you in a logical and decision-making state of mind - thus allowing you to choose a different behavior. You can reinforce this good behavior and learn from slip-ups.

***

All attitudes and behaviors are learned.

How are your thoughts and emotions tied to your behavior?

Say you really like someone. Thinking about them awakens feelings of arousal. Those are linked to loneliness (because you are not with them). Your brain has learned that pornography and masturbation are good substitutes for loneliness and will get you the pleasure you want.

Say you are super stressed out with family, school, and/or work. You haven't learned to control that stress, but your brain has learned that it can relieve the feeling of stress by using drugs.

Say you just had a fight with a loved one or you just got fired. You really don't want to think about them because you just feel so upset or hopeless. Your brain has learned that it can feel calm by turning to alcohol.

What does this knowledge do for you? Does it give you an excuse to turn to that behavior? No! It empowers you to make the correct choice when you experience those emotions.

My point is that understanding and acknowledging your emotions gives you power over them.

***

> "I know this is a touchy conversation. Being angry is okay. Yelling is not okay.

> I know we're tired and stressed. This has been a long meeting. Being frustrated is okay. Interrupting people and rolling your eyes is not okay.

> *I appreciate the passion around these different opinions and ideas. The emotion is okay. Passive-aggressive comments and put-downs are not okay."*
>
> Dare to Lead

This applies to children and their behavior. If a child displays inappropriate behavior, yes, it is the parent's job to teach them what appropriate behavior is. However, if the parent invalidates the child's emotions, it can be destructive to their growth and can lead to worse behavior. In other words, we can and should set limits on behavior, but we should not do so on emotions.

To illustrate this further, think of a child who has a favorite toy. One day, the child's toy breaks and the child starts to throw a tantrum. The child screams and cries saying he wants his toy back.

Stop and think for a second. What is the emotion behind the tantrum (behavior)? Does the child really want the toy back or to be fixed? Or does the child just need to understand the feeling of loss and learn how to overcome it? If we can see past the action (behavior) and see the emotion, we can give the proper response.

Children, like all people, have reasons for their emotions, whether they can articulate those reasons or not.

Express your emotions in a way that doesn't damage the relationship. Address the behavior but not the person's character.

It helps to look at the big picture of what's going on in their lives.

It helps to give them options they can choose.

It helps them articulate what they are feeling.

> "For many parents, recognizing children's negative emotions as opportunities for such bonding and teaching comes as a relief, a liberation, a great 'ah-ha.' We can look at our children's anger as something other than a challenge to our authority. Kids' fears are no longer evidence of our incompetence as parents. And their sadness

doesn't have to represent just 'one more blasted thing I'm going to have to fix today.'" - John M Gottman

The emotions above show how we often put ourselves first. We worry about how the emotion is affecting us rather than how the emotion is affecting the other person.

Does your child see you as an ally or an enemy? The difference is whether or not you are empathetic to their emotions.

Once you learn how emotions are tied to behavior, you can separate the two and choose your course. Recall the technique called Notice it, Name it, Find it, Flip it (NNFF). When you have the urge to turn to addictive behavior, pause and Notice what emotion you are feeling. Name it to tame it. Find its opposite. Flip your emotion to feel that way instead. By doing so (replacing the old emotion) you will no longer need the original behavior.

Here are a few examples.

Some common emotions felt when you desire to turn to an addictive behavior are: Bored, Lonely, Angry, Stressed, or Tired (BLAST). Let's see why the brain thinks addictive behaviors have a place here.

Emotion	Why addictive behavior "solves" the emotional pain
Bored	Gives you something to do
Lonely	Gives you a (false) sense of connection
Angry	Gives you a way to direct or ignore your anger
Stressed	Gives you a sense of control
Tired	Gives you something to do that doesn't require much brain power

With this understanding, let's apply the NNFF technique to choose a different behavior.

Notice and Name it	Find It	Flip It
Current Emotion	New emotion	Better solution to feel new emotion
Bored	Excited	Work on something you are passionate about and that engages the mind. Generally something that makes the world better and involves other people
Lonely	Connected	Reach out and connect to another human being - text is ok, but phone call or in person is preferred
Angry	Passionate	Release the energy in a productive way: exercise, musical instrument, crafts, etc.
Stressed	Calm	Do something simple that gives you a sense of control - something that gives a quick "win." Something that doesn't have a deadline. Breathe, puzzle, go on a walk, clear your mind, meditate, etc
Tired	Motivated	Many times being "tired" comes not from doing too much, but not doing enough of what makes you come alive. Take some deep breaths, clear your mind and do some easy movements to connect to your body (yoga, stretches, walk, etc). Then focus on something simple but productive that you enjoy doing.

These are just some examples. They all apply the principles of changing your focus and using your body to change how you feel.

Use the following table to fill in your own.

Notice and Name it	Find It	Flip It
Current Emotion	**New emotion**	**Better solution to feel new emotion**

You are aware of the emotions that you experience and why. You remember what your desires used to be. Opportunities for a brighter future have opened up to you now.

Believe you can succeed. See past the old obstacles and failures. Change is possible. Find people who have done it before or can inspire you to believe it is possible. Community and God will make it happen.

Summary of Chapter 9

Only knowledge that is used sticks.

- Merely focusing on changing behavior without addressing underlying subconscious programming can lead to frustration and self-doubt.

- Reprogramming habits is essential for sustainable change.

- All behavior is driven by emotional needs, which are normal for everyone.

Questions for Application:

- What emotional needs might be driving certain behaviors in your life? Identify a specific situation.

- How can you address these emotional needs in a positive and constructive way?

- Think about a specific goal you have. What emotional state would best support achieving this goal?

- How can you reframe the story you tell yourself about this goal to empower and motivate you?

Chapter 10 - Results: What Results Do You Get?

Progress

Strengthening of self-concept

Confidence. Happiness. Growth. Fulfillment.

This is one of the shortest chapters.

That is because if you apply everything else in this book, the results will take care of themselves. Your result is who you have become.

What have you learned while reading this book?

How do you now see yourself? Do you see yourself differently than you did before reading?

What did you learn about your beliefs?

What did you learn about your thoughts?

What did you learn about your emotions?

What did you learn about your behaviors/coping mechanisms?

How does this knowledge help you achieve the results you want?

Someone once taught me to summarize a book into three takeaways so I could always come back to my own summary if someone were to ask me about it.

What are your three takeaways?

1.

2.

3.

What are you going to do with what you have learned?

Celebrate your first downs!

Epilogue

This book is full of positive stories, inspirational messages, and a can-do attitude. It is possible to experience this flow though I fully realize that some may read this and think, "This is all great, but it doesn't apply to me because..."

You have to unlearn negative thinking. You have to reprogram your brain and rewrite your memories. Turn ghosts into ancestors. Turn failures into learning. Turn trauma into teachers.

If you get stuck in one of the sections of the model, spend some time working through it. If one layer of the model isn't working for you, go deeper. You live in your thoughts and can get stuck in your emotions. E-motion is energy that should be in motion. Unprocessed emotions can get stuck in your system, leaving you feeling weighed down. You may still be able to move forward, but it will be much easier if you take the time to work through those feelings and let them go.

What if I am Not Good Enough?

Do you believe you are enough? Or do you spend your life seeking approval from others? If you don't love yourself, you will look to others to love you. You will constantly seek external validation. That will lead you to compromise your standards for people to like you.

Kain Ramsey, a Teacher of Modern Applied Psychology said,

> "Most of us will battle at some point in our lives with thoughts and feelings which threaten to derail our success and happiness. Core beliefs include the thoughts and assumptions we hold about ourselves, others, and the world around us. They are deep-seated beliefs which often go unrecognized and yet they consistently affect our lives. Here are some common examples:

- I am unattractive

- Everyone else is better at their job than I am

- The world is full of selfish people

- Everyone just wants to take and never give

> Of the many limiting beliefs that hold people back in life, the big kahuna is: 'I'm Not Good Enough.' These words make up the internal dialogue of almost every person on the face of the planet. If they resonate with you, you're definitely not alone! Somewhere along the way, we bought into the idea that we weren't good enough, so we decided that we would try and become perfect, which is an endless, tireless pursuit."

Once this belief of "I'm not good enough" is formed we continually look for ways to validate and prove that it's true. For example:

My parents didn't stay together = There's something wrong with me = I'm not good enough

Someone's not interested in me = There's something wrong with me = I'm not good enough

I didn't get the job I wanted = There's something wrong with me = I'm not good enough

This pattern of habitual thinking can follow us right through the extent of our lives if we allow it to.

As we begin to think differently and take ownership of new ideas, we can change the way we think, change the way we interpret the past, and change and modify our expectations of the future. If we're simply bold enough to accept the fact that we as individuals are "good enough" – not perfect – but "good enough," then this sets us free for the rest of our lives.

We no longer have to strive for perfection and can simply just commit to a journey of self-improvement, where we work on being a better version of ourselves today than what we were yesterday and so on.

I am enough. I am just trying to be better.

Consider the events from your past where you learned to believe you were "not good enough." How might you reinterpret these events now?

This fear of not being good enough can be rooted in something specific from your past or it could be a belief you have come to accept over the years. Either way, to root something out, you must do what is being taught in this book. Shine a light on the fear so you can dispel it. Many of the tools in this book will help you do that on your own. But if you need help, please reach out. It is worth it.

If your sense of identity is tainted (you feel you aren't good enough, something is wrong with you, you are labeled a certain way and are therefore "less than") you may start to think solutions offered in this book aren't for you. This all comes from results-dependent thinking ("I tried it and it didn't work"). Seek help to work through your emotions and challenge your negative thoughts so you can rewrite your limiting beliefs and see yourself for who you really are.

Lauren Daigle wrote a powerful song that addresses the feelings of not being enough:

I keep fighting voices in my mind that say I'm not enough

Every single lie that tells me I will never measure up

Am I more than just the sum of every high and every low?

Remind me once again just who I am, because I need to know,

(Chorus)

You say I am loved when I can't feel a thing

You say I am strong when I think I am weak

And You say I am held when I am falling short

And when I don't belong, oh, You say I am Yours

And I believe (I), oh, I believe (I) What You say of me (I) I believe

The only thing that matters now is everything You think of me In You I find my worth, in You I find my identity,

(Chorus repeats)

Taking all I have and now I'm layin' it at Your feet

You'll have every failure God, You'll have every victory,

You say I am loved when I can't feel a thing

You say I am strong when I think I am weak

You say I am held when I am falling short

When I don't belong, oh, You say I am Yours

And I believe (I), oh, I believe (I) What You say of me (I) I believe

What is your takeaway from these lyrics?

Will God ever tell you that you are not good enough? He definitely won't. So ask Him to fill your empty spots with His love. Let Him heal you. God can help you know you are good enough and He wants to help you.

You are good enough.

That being said, I knew a girl who had a hard time believing that.

I once gave a presentation on overcoming emotional pain to a group of young adults. As I shared my story, the subject of God and how He can heal our pain came up. One of the girls in the audience all of a sudden clammed up and had a hard time participating after that. Her one comment the whole night was that she was taught to "just rub some dirt in it" when it came to emotional pain.

She is another one of the people who is super popular and seems extremely happy with life. But deep down she was hurting to the point where she struggled to connect to others.

I spoke to her after class and discovered that she had a hard time relating to the class when we started talking about God because she felt so distanced from Him. She said she was doing all the right things like going to church, praying, and reading scriptures, but she just didn't feel anything.

I told her that I could certainly relate because I had gone through a similar experience.

When we have gone so long suppressing our unpleasant emotions, we also suppress our pleasant emotions. In other words, we grow numb to feelings. Because we have numbed our feelings, it is harder to feel what we think we should feel at church or when we pray.

Unfortunately, I haven't had the opportunity to work with this person as a client, but I encouraged her to reach out to someone and I do know she started to talk to her parents and trusted leaders and began to feel much better and make some good progress.

She learned two lessons that can also be helpful to you.

1. She is not alone when she is worried about why she doesn't feel the way she thinks she should.

2. She learned the importance of reaching out and talking to a trusted person about where she is.

We are taught that God can heal all afflictions and diseases. That includes emotional, mental, and spiritual. Once we believe that Christ can heal us, we begin the healing process.

The hole I talk about is we might believe we are not worth healing.

The solution here is to study the doctrine of the relationship between us and God. If you can remember that you are a child of God you will dispel the idea that you are a problem and not worth healing.

I just needed it much more plainly (or simply in a different way) and I believe many others do as well.

My story was where I believed Christ could help everyone but me. I thought I was alone.

Why would that happen? Could it be because I had so many unresolved emotions and I didn't understand how Christ could make me feel better?

The voice in my head was telling me that because I didn't feel what I thought I should feel at church or in life, God must not care about me. "My feelings are real! All the signs are there!" Yes, but that doesn't make it true. I had to realize that I wasn't the problem. I had to realize where those voices were coming from so I could fight the real enemy.

Once I knew who the real enemy was (not me, but the devil putting thoughts inside my head) I stopped fighting myself and thinking I was not good enough. I understood that God was on my side this whole time and if I teamed up with Him, I could expel the devil from my mind.

The truth will set you free. Once you know the truth, it will be easier to make the right decision. To know your enemy is to beat your enemy.

One of Satan's most effective strategies is to convince you that he doesn't exist and that you are the problem. If he can make you feel broken and worthless, he can take you out of the fight. He will crush your self-esteem by telling you that there is something wrong with you that cannot be fixed and that you are not loved or good enough. Satan uses these lies to try and distance you from God, making you question His love for you and lose faith in your future.

When you have thoughts like, "I am not worth anything. I am not good enough" know that those are lies straight from the devil and you can tell him where to go. Label your thoughts as "from Satan" or "from God." You are worth healing and can be healed. Not only can you be healed, but you can be powerful. (I use the term "healed" because I thought I was broken and needed healing. Even though you aren't broken, it can take time for your feelings to heal and you feel whole.)

So don't distance yourself from God. Don't leave the Lord out of your life. Pray and read the scriptures when you need help. When you are desperate for help, turn to Him. It is during those times that you truly learn to rely on Him. He has to teach you that it is only He who can perform the miracles you need. You need Him and He is happy to help.

The times that you are at a loss of what to do are the times you can fully turn to the Lord and allow Him to help you. This is when the Lord can make more of you than you could by yourself.

"With Me, all things are possible."

God never left me and He never stopped caring about me. I was listening to the wrong voice in my head and had numbed my feelings.

Remember where the thoughts in your mind are coming from and know that you always have the power to choose which ones you listen to.

When you think you are not good enough, you can challenge that thought.

What emotions will come if you think you are not good enough? Self-doubt, loneliness, shame, etc? If a thought enters your mind and makes you worried, ask yourself, "Where did that thought come from?" If it came from Satan, expel it. Don't give it one more thought. You choose how you feel by challenging your thoughts.

Although you may feel like you are the only one who isn't good enough, know that everyone feels that way at some point in their life.

Consider the following:

A singer sold 5 million albums.

A speaker presented to 500,000 people.

A leader has 7,000 in his Facebook group.

Who is "better" here? Everything is relative. Are any of those numbers "good enough?" How do you know when you "made it?" If you are always comparing yourself to others, of course you will feel that you aren't good enough. It is natural for you to compare your worst with someone else's best. Comparison destroys self-confidence and the belief that you are enough. So just don't compare.

But knowing that you aren't alone in feeling this way – just getting it off your chest – helps you realize it isn't just you. You aren't the problem.

Just because things haven't worked out doesn't mean things won't work out.

Your past doesn't equal your future.

Your past does not define you, but it can refine you.

You are a warrior. If Satan can get in your head and make you think you aren't good enough, he has conquered the warrior from within. You don't want to be taken out of the battle! You are still needed! You can still make a difference!

Never forget that your true worth never changes. You are a child of God. He has a plan for you. He knows what is truly important. Trust Him.

Others believing in you

Sometimes we are asked to do something we don't feel qualified to do or we don't have a clue where to start. Perhaps we just don't believe in ourselves or that we can do it.

I have felt this way many times. One of those times was when I was the HR intern at a quickly growing company. My manager was leaving more and more up to me but I didn't have any experience with those aspects of HR, let alone in different states and countries! There was nobody to tell me the right way to do things and I was left to answer questions on my own.

One of the leaders sat me down one day and told me I just needed to have confidence in my decisions. He was confident that my decisions were good. I just needed to learn that for myself.

Because he believed in me, I began to believe in myself. I began to believe that I could do anything that was asked of me. It made me want to succeed for him as well.

When somebody who means a lot to you believes in you, your confidence level goes up exponentially.

I had another leader who never doubted me. He always had full confidence in me. I knew that because he never made me feel dumb – rather, he helped me see past a mistake and helped me move forward. His belief in me made me believe I could do anything he needed. It made me want to do anything he asked.

Have you had an experience where you had someone believe in you and it made all the difference?

Sometimes your belief in someone can make all the difference.

If you give someone an expectation you believe they already live up to, they will do everything they can to live up to that.

Believe in your kids and they will believe in themselves. Teach them that mistakes can be fixed. No shame in them. Treat them kindly too.

Be the believer.

How to believe in yourself when you think you have reason not to

Let's first go over some possible reasons why you would think you have a reason not to believe in yourself:

- You have acted against your values and now have a guilty conscience

- You compare yourself to others

- Something from your past has convinced you that you are broken or worthless

- You feel you have been trying so hard for so long and just feel like a failure

What is your reason?

I invite you to be completely honest with yourself and learn to see that reason but be ready to challenge it. Is that reason truly valid or is it actually an unresolved emotion linked to a limiting belief?

There have been times in my life when I have made mistakes and I felt like there was no coming back. I felt I had done something so bad nobody could ever love me.

Even after having gone through recovery and having learned all sorts of proper tools to keep me strong, I made the same mistake again. Boy did I feel stupid after that. "I should have known better! In fact, I did know better!"

Then I started to really beat myself up. I didn't need anyone to tell me I did something wrong. I already knew!

How do you come out of this?

Forgiveness is needed when someone doesn't meet your expectations, be it yourself or others.

This has to do with how we view our failures and the past experiences that have tainted our vision of ourselves and given us limiting beliefs. It leads us to think we're not good enough, that it is too hard, or that it will never work out, which causes emotional pain. If you don't love yourself and heal from the hurt, you will lead your life and others from hurt and fear. Hurt people often hurt other people. You usually end up treating people how you are treating yourself.

Your feelings don't define who you are, but if left unresolved they will affect your life in ways you could have avoided. By processing your emotions correctly, you can become better rather than bitter. You can choose to rise from the hurt stronger, or carry on with grudges - the choice is yours.

Take responsibility for your present so you can have a better future.

Love takes time. Love of self takes time.

Forgive yourself and anyone else who has harmed you.

People just want to feel better about themselves. If you love them, believe in them, and see what is best in them, they will leave feeling better about themselves. This works for you as well.

You are never more than one day away from a new life.

Take responsibility for your thoughts, feelings, and behaviors - no one else can. Then you can move on. Don't define yourself by it as making you broken. You are not the only one who has made a mistake.

The same principles we have discussed in this entire book apply here. Surround yourself with good people. Do not isolate. Isolation invites shame to be your roommate.

Reach out and talk to God, trusted family and friends, and maybe even professional help. Truly, there is a light at the end of this tunnel and the sooner you face your emotions and let them out, the sooner you can move on from how you are feeling right now.

It is natural to "feel dumb" for having put yourself in that situation that caused the emotional pain. Just know you can get through it and it doesn't have to define you.

If you feel the desire to love yourself but just struggle to even believe it is possible, you can work with a desire to believe.

In Mark 9 we read the account of a father who begs Christ to heal his son who had a dumb spirit in him since childhood. The father had previously asked the disciples to heal his boy but they could not. The father says to Christ, "If you canst do anything, have compassion on us, and help us." Christ replies with, "If thou canst believe, all things are possible to him that believeth." The next verse says, "And straightway the father of the child cried out, and said with tears, 'Lord, I believe; help thou mine unbelief.'"

Can you feel the desire of the father in this story? He recognized someone who could help. He had tried to help rid his son of this spirit since childhood. Now, when Christ tells him his boy can be healed if he can just believe, he "straightway" cried out and "said with tears" the desire of his heart.

When the man asks Christ for help, he first says, "I believe" but then follows with a fully honest, "Help thou mine unbelief." Christ then rebukes the spirit and it leaves the boy's body.

Notice three things here: First, even when the tools available to man have not succeeded, you can always reach out to God and know that He will help. Second, it requires you to be fully honest with yourself and with God. Third, when you are honest and humble, you are then ready for the Lord to perform a miracle.

"Help thou mine unbelief." Perhaps that means, "Thou knowest that I *want* to believe, but I have something holding me back. I have this foul spirit, this limiting belief, these negative thoughts, or this emotional pain. Please help me with that.

Please.

I beg you.

I have no one else I can talk to about it."

This is what a simple, yet powerful, desire to learn to love yourself can bring you.

The more you love yourself, the less sensitive you are to what others think of you. You are confident in yourself and are able to help others strengthen their self-confidence.

Don't let the reactions of others determine whether you feel loved or not. Your source of self-esteem should not come from others but from a confidence born of God.

Knowing how it feels when you experience God's love is so important and knowing what you can do to increase the frequency of that feeling is important because <u>your capacity to experience His love is the model for how well you love others.</u>

Why does God always respond in Love? Because He knows if you feel His love you will want to do what He says. He also knows that by following His commandments we will feel His love. In other words, rather than make you feel bad for not following a commandment you already know you should follow, He loves you. He validates you and your emotions. He makes sure you know you aren't broken and that you are worthy of being loved. That is the greatest motivation to change.

How do you learn to love someone? You spend time with them. You are honest and vulnerable with them. You work through differences and forgive when mistakes are made. Do you think this only applies when you are learning to love another person? Or could it also apply to learning to love yourself?

When do I feel loved? When I slow down enough to hear and feel it.

We all long to feel validated, acknowledged, accepted, encouraged, and loved.

How do you learn to love yourself?

By what you focus on and the story you tell yourself.

How would someone else feel if you talked to them the way you talk to yourself? Do you focus on what is wrong or what is missing or on what you have and are working towards?

Focusing on what you don't desire in life brings feelings of shame and anxiety.

Focusing on what you do desire brings motivation and excitement.

Is your sense of worth based on your results, outcomes, or performance? If so, what happens when those aren't what you want them to be? You can't define yourself by things that change (title, position, income, performance, feedback, preferences, grade, etc.)

If your sense of worth is determined by whether you have a girlfriend or boyfriend, you will always seek to be in a relationship but will be crushed if it falls apart.

If you define yourself by your title at work or your social position at school, what happens when you lose your job or leave that school?

You must learn to love yourself independent of any title, label, status, result, feedback, etc.

This comes from a true understanding of who you are at the core.

Love your current self. Don't judge yourself of yesterday by the knowledge you have today. You know better now so you can do better now.

Love yourself by forgiving yourself. Forgive yourself so you can love yourself.

We take care of our dental health more than our mental health. Practice self-love like brushing your teeth. Every day. In fact, when you are brushing your teeth, actually look in the mirror and actually look yourself in the eyes. Tell yourself some positive things about yourself. Have a personal compliment session.

Now that you love yourself, focus on loving others.

When we see ourselves as loveable, good enough, capable, powerful, and every other thing that God sees in us, we can truly reach our ultimate potential and achieve lasting results and fulfillment.

Would you like more from this author? Follow him at any of the following:

www.reachyourultimatepotential.com

www.facebook.com/benedenspeaks

www.instagram.com/benedenspeaks

YouTube: Ben Eden Speaks

Reach Your Ultimate Potential Podcast

Who do you know that needs to know this?

Awesome! Now go share this with someone.

If you enjoyed this book, I would appreciate a 5-star review on Amazon.

Appendix

E xamples of the model applied

Results	Consequence if you aren't "successful"
Lose weight	You are judged (or you judge yourself)
Earn money	You are discouraged and have low self esteem.
Grow your business	You feel frustrated and anxious.
Get married	You are lonely

Results	Behavior	Consequence if you aren't "successful"
Lose weight	Workout. Diet	Try something else (a different behavior)
Earn money	Work hard. Get a job. Get a degree.	Get a different job. Get another degree.
Grow your business	Work long hours. Network. Sell.	Work harder. Invest in more advertising.
Get married	Go on dates.	Go on more dates.

Results	Behavior	Emotions of pain	Emotions of pleasure	Consequence if you aren't "successful"
Lose weight	Workout. Diet	Overwhelmed, anxious, discouraged	Excited, motivated, passionate, etc	You think you are the only one that feels this way and you now can't tell anyone.
Earn money	Work hard. Get a job. Get a degree.	Overwhelmed, anxious, discouraged	Excited, motivated, passionate, etc	You are discouraged and unmotivated
Grow your business	Work long hours. Network. Sell.	Overwhelmed, anxious, discouraged	Excited, motivated, passionate, etc	You are discouraged and unmotivated
Get married	Go on dates.	Overwhelmed, anxious, discouraged	Excited, motivated, passionate, etc	You are discouraged and unmotivated

Results	Behavior	Emotions of pain	Emotions of pleasure	Thoughts Avoid Pain	Thoughts Gain pleasure	Consequence if you aren't "successful"
Lose weight	Workout. Diet	Overwhelmed, anxious, discouraged	Excited, motivated, passionate, etc	This is too hard. I am tired. I'll try harder next time.	I can do this! This is working. I see progress.	You start to have thoughts like, "Why isn't this working? Why are others more successful than me?"
Earn money	Work hard. Get a job. Get a degree.	Overwhelmed, anxious, discouraged	Excited, motivated, passionate, etc	This is too hard. I am tired. I'll try harder next time.	I can do this! This is working. I see progress.	You start to have thoughts like, "Why isn't this working? Why are others more successful than me?"
Grow your business	Work long hours. Network. Sell.	Overwhelmed, anxious, discouraged	Excited, motivated, passionate, etc	This is too hard. I am tired. I'll try harder tomorrow.	I can do this! This is working. I see progress.	You start to have thoughts like, "Why isn't this working? Why are others more successful than me?"
Get married	Go on dates.	Overwhelmed, anxious, discouraged	Excited, motivated, passionate, etc	This is too hard. I am tired. I'll try harder later.	I can do this! This is working. I see progress.	You start to have thoughts like, "Why isn't this working? Why are others more successful than me?"

APPENDIX

Results	Behavior	Emotion Avoid pain	Emotion Gain pleasure	Thoughts Avoid Pain	Thoughts Gain pleasure	Beliefs Disempowering or Limited	Beliefs Empowering	Consequence if you aren't "successful"
Lose weight	Workout. Diet	Overwhelmed, anxious, discouraged	Excited, motivated, passionate, etc	This is too hard. I am tired. I'll try harder next time.	This is working. I see progress.	I can't do this. This will never work.	I can do this! I feel great in my body and have all the energy I need.	You reinforce the belief that you can't do it. "See? I knew I wasn't good enough. I am just not cut out for this."
Earn money	Work hard. Get a job. Get a degree.	Overwhelmed, anxious, discouraged	Excited, motivated, passionate, etc	This is too hard. I am tired. I'll try harder next time.	This is working. I see progress.	I can't do this. This will never work.	I participate in the flow of money and have all that I need.	You reinforce the belief that you can't do it. "See? I knew I wasn't good enough. I am just not cut out for this."
Grow your business	Work long hours. Network. Sell.	Overwhelmed, anxious, discouraged	Excited, motivated, passionate, etc	This is too hard. I am tired. I'll try harder next time.	This is working. I see progress.	I can't do this. This will never work.	My daily efforts allow many people to receive value from my services.	You reinforce the belief that you can't do it. "See? I knew I wasn't good enough. I am just not cut out for this."
Get married	Go on dates.	Overwhelmed, anxious, discouraged	Excited, motivated, passionate, etc	This is too hard. I am tired. I'll try harder next time.	This is working. I see progress.	I can't do this. This will never work.	I am living in a way to attract the right person at the right time.	You reinforce the belief that you can't do it. "See? I knew I wasn't good enough. I am just not cut out for this."

Results	Behavior	Emotion Avoid pain	Emotion Gain pleasure	Thoughts Avoid Pain	Thoughts Gain pleasure	Beliefs Disempowering or Limited	Beliefs Empowering	Identity	Consequence if you aren't "successful"
Lose weight	Workout. Diet	Overwhelmed, anxious, discouraged	Excited, motivated, passionate, etc	This is too hard. I am tired. I'll try harder next time.	This is working. I see progress.	I can't do this. This will never work.	I can do this! I feel great in my body and have all the energy I need.	I am healthy. I am energetic.	There is no consequence because if you know your identity, you can't "fail" at it.
Earn money	Work hard. Get a job. Get a degree.	Overwhelmed, anxious, discouraged	Excited, motivated, passionate, etc	This is too hard. I am tired. I'll try harder next time.	This is working. I see progress.	I can't do this. This will never work	I participate in the flow of money and have all that I need.	I am happy, wealthy, and wise.	There is no consequence because if you know your identity, you can't "fail" at it.
Grow your business	Work long hours. Network. Sell.	Overwhelmed, anxious, discouraged	Excited, motivated, passionate, etc	This is too hard. I am tired. I'll try harder next time.	This is working. I see progress.	I can't do this. This will never work.	My daily efforts allow many people to receive value from my services.	I am a business owner.	There is no consequence because if you know your identity, you can't "fail" at it.
Get married	Go on dates.	Overwhelmed, anxious, discouraged	Excited, motivated, passionate, etc	This is too hard. I am tired. I'll try harder next time.	This is working. I see progress.	I can't do this. This will never work.	I am living in a way to attract the right person at the right time.	I am a husband or wife.	There is no consequence because if you know your identity, you can't "fail" at it.

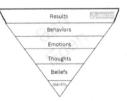

The Eden Model

Questions to help with the model:

What will I get?

What do I have to do?

What do I feel?

What do I think?

What do I believe?

How do I see myself?

What do I want?

What do I have to do?

What do I have to feel?

What do I have to think?

What do I have to believe?

Who will I have to be?

What am I getting?

What am I doing?

What am I feeling?

What am I thinking?

What do I believe?

How do I see myself? Who am I?

More examples of how this model works:

I am a problem solver.

I am confident I can solve this problem.

I come up with ideas on how to solve the problem.

I am excited about those ideas.

I implement the ideas.

I get the results.

Thoughts (this is where you have the most control)

Emotions (the better you can manage this (by managing your thoughts) the better you will manage your life

Behavior (this is what everyone stresses)

Results (this is what everyone wants or sees)

Questions to help you focus on and assign new meaning in each section:

Sense of self: Now that I know what thoughts are coming from the devil, what do I know about myself from God? What are my strengths, values, and characteristics?

Thoughts: What are my options? Where are these thoughts coming from? Is this thought true? If so, what is the evidence that it is an accurate thought? If it is not accurate, what alternative thought can I have?

Emotions: What emotion am I feeling right now? What thoughts are causing this? How would I like to feel instead? What can I do right now to feel that way?

Behavior: What am I trying to achieve? What emotional need am I trying to meet?

Results: What results do I want here? What must I believe in order to achieve these results?

Kids bond through play. They like to have fun and feel safe with you. Then they will open up. They don't realize this process is happening, but here is what is happening in their brain:

Do I trust you with my behavior? Will I do what you ask?

Do I trust you with my emotions? Will I be vulnerable with you?

Do I trust you with my thoughts? Will I share my concerns and questions with you?

Do I trust you with my self-concept? Do I know you have my best interests in mind and can help me become a better person?

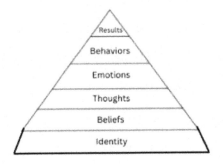

Pyramid Level	Description
Results	What you get
Behaviors	What you do
Emotions	What you feel
Thoughts	What you think
Beliefs	What you believe
Identity	What you see

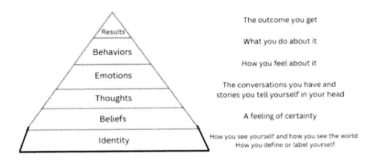

Pyramid Level	Description
Results	The outcome you get
Behaviors	What you do about it
Emotions	How you feel about it
Thoughts	The conversations you have and stories you tell yourself in your head
Beliefs	A feeling of certainty
Identity	How you see yourself and how you see the world. How you define or label yourself

REFERENCES

Robbins, Tony. How to breakthrough to success. https://www.tonyrobbins.com/podcasts/3-steps-breakthrough/. Accessed Nov 8, 2023.

Duhigg, Charles. The Power of Habit. Random House Books, 2013.

Clear, James. Atomic Habits: An Easy and Proven Way to Build Habits and Break Bad Ones. Penguin Random House, 2018

Gottman, J. M., & DeClaire, J. Raising an emotionally intelligent child. New York, N.Y., Simon & Schuster Paperbacks, 1997

The Hans Christian Andersen Center. andersen.sdu.dk/vaerk/hersholt/TheEmperorsNewClothes_e.html September 19, 2019

Goldy–gry. Joy and Sadness. www.deviantart.com/goldy--gry/art/Joy-and-Sadness-542687290. 2015

Mason, Daryn. CX Shorts: The Elephant and Rope. www.linkedin.com/pulse/cx-shorts-elephant-rope-daryn-mason/.2017

Nelson, Dr. Bradley. The Emotion Code: How to Release Your Trapped Emotions for Abundant Health, Love, and Happiness, St. Martin's Publishing Group, 2019

Brown, Brene. Dare to Lead. Vermilion, 2018

Carnegie, Dale. How to Stop Worrying and Start Living. Pocket, 1990

Okamura. Medium. okamuraglobal.medium.com/davis-smith-the-ceo-of-cotopaxi-called-next-patagonia-a15760878c#:~:text=Cotopaxi%20is%20called%20%E2%80%9Cthe%20next,go%20back%20to%20Davis's%20roots. 2021

Daigle, Lauren. You Say. www.google.com/search?q=lyrics+to+you+say+by+lauren+daigle&rlz

=1C1CHKZ_enUS430US430&oq=lyrics+to+you+say&aqs=chrome.
1.69i57j0l7.4151j0j1&sourceid=chrome&ie=UTF-8. 2018

Vince Popale. www.vincepapale.com/realstory.htm. 2020

Erwin, Andrew, and Jon Erwin. I Can Only Imagine. Lions Gate Entertainment, Santa Monica, CA, 2018

Docter, Pete, and Ronnie Del Carmen. Inside Out. Walt Disney Studios Motion Pictures, 2015.

Winch, Guy. 5 ways emotional pain is worse. www.psychologytoday.com/us/blog/the-squeaky-wheel/2014 07/5-ways-emotional-pain-is-worse-physical-pain. 2014

Szalavitz, Maia. Unbroken Brain: A Revolutionary New Way of Understanding Addiction. New York, St. Martin's Press, 2016.

Frankl, Viktor E. (Viktor Emil), 1905-1997, author. Man's Search for Meaning : an Introduction to Logotherapy. Boston :Beacon Press, 1962.

Izadi, Elahe. Why life is beautiful, according to this 92-year-old Holocaust survivor. https://www.washingtonpost.com/news/inspired-life/wp/2016/04/07/why-life-is-beautiful-according-to-this-92-year-old-holocaust-survivor/. 2016

Baime, WWI's Christmas Truce: When Fighting Paused for the Holiday https://www.history.com/news/christmas-truce-1914-world-war-i-soldier-accounts. 2018